THE BL

NOTES

including
- *Life and Background of the Author*
- *Introductions to the Novels*
- *Lists of Characters*
- *Brief Synopses*
- *Critical Commentaries*
- *Character Analyses*
- *Critical Essays*
- *Genealogies*
- *Review Questions and Essay Topics*
- *Selected Bibliography*

by
Rosetta James, B.A.   *and*   Louisa S. Nye, M.A.
Teacher of English   Old Dominion University
New York City

Wiley Publishing, Inc.

Editor
Gary Carey, M.A., University of Colorado

Consulting Editor
James L. Roberts, Ph.D., Department of
English, University of Nebraska

CliffsNotes™ *The Bluest Eye & Sula*

Published by:
Wiley Publishing, Inc.
909 Third Avenue
New York, NY 10022
www.wiley.com

Note: If you purchased this book without a cover, you should be aware that this book is stolen property. It was reported as "unsold and destroyed" to the publisher, and neither the author nor the publisher has received any payment for this "stripped book."

Copyright © 1997 Wiley Publishing, Inc., New York, New York
ISBN: 0-8220-0251-5
Printed in the United States of America
10
1O/RQ/QS/QT/IN
Published by Wiley Publishing, Inc., New York, NY
Published simultaneously in Canada
No part of this publication may be reproduced, stored in a retrieval system, or transmitted in any form or by any means, electronic, mechanical, photocopying, recording, scanning, or otherwise, except as permitted under Sections 107 or 108 of the 1976 United States Copyright Act, without either the prior written permission of the Publisher, or authorization through payment of the appropriate per-copy fee to the Copyright Clearance Center, 222 Rosewood Drive, Danvers, MA 01923, 978-750-8400, fax 978-750-4470. Requests to the Publisher for permission should be addressed to the Legal Department, Wiley Publishing, Inc., 10475 Crosspoint Blvd., Indianapolis, IN 46256, 317-572-3447, fax 317-572-4447, or e-mail permcoordinator@wiley.com

LIMIT OF LIABILITY/DISCLAIMER OF WARRANTY: THE PUBLISHER AND AUTHOR HAVE USED THEIR BEST EFFORTS IN PREPARING THIS BOOK. THE PUBLISHER AND AUTHOR MAKE NO REPRESENTATIONS OR WARRANTIES WITH RESPECT TO THE ACCURACY OR COMPLETENESS OF THE CONTENTS OF THIS BOOK AND SPECIFICALLY DISCLAIM ANY IMPLIED WARRANTIES OF MERCHANTABILITY OR FITNESS FOR A PARTICULAR PURPOSE. THERE ARE NO WARRANTIES WHICH EXTEND BEYOND THE DESCRIPTIONS CONTAINED IN THIS PARAGRAPH. NO WARRANTY MAY BE CREATED OR EXTENDED BY SALES REPRESENTATIVES OR WRITTEN SALES MATERIALS. THE ACCURACY AND COMPLETENESS OF THE INFORMATION PROVIDED HEREIN AND THE OPINIONS STATED HEREIN ARE NOT GUARANTEED OR WARRANTED TO PRODUCE ANY PARTICULAR RESULTS, AND THE ADVICE AND STRATEGIES CONTAINED HEREIN MAY NOT BE SUITABLE FOR EVERY INDIVIDUAL. NEITHER THE PUBLISHER NOR AUTHOR SHALL BE LIABLE FOR ANY LOSS OF PROFIT OR ANY OTHER COMMERCIAL DAMAGES, INCLUDING BUT NOT LIMITED TO SPECIAL, INCIDENTAL, CONSEQUENTIAL, OR OTHER DAMAGES.

Trademarks: Wiley, the Wiley Publishing logo, Cliffs, CliffsNotes, the CliffsNotes logo, CliffsAP, CliffsComplete, CliffsTestPrep, CliffsQuickReview, CliffsNote-a-Day and all related logos and trade dress are registered trademarks or trademarks of Wiley Publishing, Inc., in the United States and other countries. All other trademarks are property of their respective owners. Wiley Publishing, Inc., is not associated with any product or vendor mentioned in this book.

For general information on our other products and services or to obtain technical support, please contact our Customer Care Department within the U.S. at 800-762-2974, outside the U.S. at 317-572-3993, or fax 317-572-4002.

Wiley also publishes its books in a variety of electronic formats. Some content that appears in print may not be available in electronic books.

CONTENTS

Life and Background of the Author 5

The Bluest Eye

Introduction to the Novel 9
List of Characters 11
A Brief Synopsis 15
Structure of *The Bluest Eye* 18
Critical Commentaries 19
Character Analyses 37
Critical Essay 41
Review Questions and Essay Topics 43

Sula

Introduction to the Novel 45
List of Characters 46
A Brief Synopsis 48
Critical Commentaries 50
Character Analyses 84
Critical Essays 87
Review Questions and Essay Topics 94

Selected Bibliography 95

Center Spread: *The Bluest Eye* and *Sula* Genealogies

THE BLUEST EYE

Notes

LIFE AND BACKGROUND OF THE AUTHOR

Childhood to Womanhood. Although she grew up in the North, southern traditions played a large part in Toni Morrison's upbringing. Her maternal grandfather, a Kentucky carpenter and farmer, saw no chance for advancement because of the state's racism and poverty, so he moved his family to Ohio. From them, Morrison absorbed stories and tales about the horrors of black life during the Reconstruction era—roughly, the twelve years following the Civil War—when the southern states that seceded from the Union were politically restructured and economically restored. She recognized that "whatever I did was easy in comparison with what they had to go through."

Morrison's father, sharecropper George Wofford, had similar reasons to escape racial oppression in Georgia and relocate in the North. Even there, however, he distrusted "every word and every gesture of every white man on earth." In contrast, Morrison's mother, Ramah, a more educated, trusting person than her husband, was a gentler, less confrontational parent to young Chloe Anthony Wofford, who would become world-renowned Toni Morrison, 1993 winner of the Nobel Prize for Literature.

The second of four children, Morrison was born on February 18, 1931, and grew up on the far western fringe of Cleveland, in the multicultural environment of Lorain, Ohio—a steel town of around 75,000, blending Czech, German, Irish, Greek, Italian, Serb, Mexican, and black suburbanites. There, she experienced exclusion but did not suffer the intense racism felt by such black writers as Maya Angelou, Dick Gregory, and Richard Wright.

Brought up in a nurturing, religious environment, Morrison says, "We were taught that as individuals we had value, irrespective of what the future might hold for us." The women of the black community, whether aunts, grandmothers, or neighbors, served as a tightly woven safety net. The oral tradition, passed down by both men and women, cushioned blows to self-esteem with stories and songs about the Underground Railroad, daring rescues, and other perils and triumphs of black history.

Morrison was expected to excel, even though she had to contend with the racial prejudice that accompanied growing up in an educational system that ignored the contributions of nonwhites. At Lorain High School, she graduated at the top of her class, then surprised her family by insisting on leaving Lorain to obtain a college degree—a decision that necessitated her father working three jobs. The move from Ohio alarmed her mother; all of her daughter's friends and relatives were in Ohio. Self-assured about her ambitions, Morrison has remarked, "You take the village with you. There is no need for the community if you have a sense of it inside."

Morrison entered Howard University in Washington, D.C., changed her first name from Chloe to Toni, and began studying under strong African-American spokesmen, including poet Sterling Brown and philosopher and critic Alain Locke, a Rhodes scholar who edited *The New Negro*. She graduated with a B.A. in 1953 and completed a master's degree in English at Cornell two years later, with a concentration in the works of Virginia Woolf and William Faulkner.

Teaching and Writing. In 1957, Morrison taught humanities and English at Texas Southern University, then worked for eight years as an English instructor at Howard University. In 1966, she joined a monthly literary symposium and contributed stories that she had begun in high school. Among them was a story she read aloud to the symposium about a black girl who wanted to make up for her so-called physical shortcomings—her strong Negroid features—by petitioning God for blue eyes.

From 1965 to 1983, Morrison served as a textbook editor at Random House, in Syracuse, New York. Divorced, raising two small sons, and working at a full-time, demanding job, she still managed to plug away at *The Bluest Eye*, her personal therapy for depression and isolation. Explaining her drive to write, Morrison has said that she had a deep need for "books that I had wanted to read. No one had written them yet, so I wrote them." She has said this about her compulsion to complete her first manuscript: "I had no will, no judgment, no perspective, no power, no authority, no self—just this brutal sense of irony, melancholy, and a trembling respect for words. I wrote like someone with a dirty habit. Secretly—compulsively—slyly."

By the time the manuscript for *The Bluest Eye* was complete in 1968, Morrison had risen to the rank of senior editor at Random House's publishing headquarters in New York City. According to her, her first novel sold for racial reasons: Random House wanted a black writer in its stable.

A year later, she returned to the classroom for a year as the Albert Schweitzer Professor of Humanities at State University of New York in Purchase, settled into a renovated boathouse outside Nyack, and continued to write. Four years later, she completed *Sula*, her second novel, which continues her demarcation of the black woman's world, with its secret power, perversity, unity, and mysticism. The critics were divided about the horror of a mother's murdering her drug-addicted son: To some, the act was unforgivable; to others, the woman exhibited a mother's utmost love and courage. What none of the critics could have foreseen, however, was that Morrison's portrait of the drug-addicted son was an omen of ghetto life in the coming decades.

In 1974, an attraction to the lodestone of black literature led her to compile a memory album. Introduced by Bill Cosby as a "folk journey of Black America" and composed of bits and pieces from slave narratives, advertising, photographs, media clippings, recipes, and patent office records, *The Black Book* reveals three centuries of black history. Almost like remediation in the culture that her public education had denied her, the research, her "literary archeology," provided a cache of motifs, themes, and images for later fiction— including a clipping from a nineteenth-century magazine that would inspire *Beloved*.

During the next decade, while serving as a visiting lecturer at Yale, she finished *Song of Solomon* (1977), a Midwestern saga. Like a patchwork vision of her collective unconscious, the novel draws on family lore and a wisdom sprung from surviving. In Morrison's words, her forebears became "my entrance into my own interior life." True to the revelation of self, *Song of Solomon*, a mythic tale centering on slaves who fly to Africa, evolved from her grief over her father's death. The novel was awarded the 1978 National

Book Critics Circle Award for fiction, and eighteen years later, in 1996, it soared to the No. 1 position on bestseller lists nationwide when it was announced as a featured novel in Oprah [Winfrey]'s monthly book club.

Within four years after *Solomon*'s success, Morrison followed up with *Tar Baby*. A provocative departure from her earlier all-black casts, the novel introduces the ambivalent Jadine, a world-weary traveler who searches for self-actualization among West Indian servant-caste relatives through a brief fling with a furtive black interloper. Propelled by the novel's success, Morrison became the first black woman championed in a cover story for *Newsweek*, which heralded her as the top black writer in the United States. Her response was a teasing one-liner: "Are you really going to put a middle-aged, gray-haired, colored lady on the cover of this magazine?"

Beloved, her masterwork thus far, was published in 1987. Returning to a focus on motherhood, the novel probes the pain of mothers who are slaves, revealed through the humiliation of Sethe, who kills one of her children rather than watch it grow to adulthood, when she would be brutally and repeatedly punished, robbed of a sense of self, and utterly debased by slavery.

In January 1988, having worked her way up in the literary hierarchy, Morrison received the Ritz-Hemingway, National Book, and National Book Critics Circle nominations for *Beloved*—but no awards. Led by poet June Jordan, a formal protest that white critics were unwilling to recognize Morrison's enormous talent ran in major newspapers, accompanied by an open letter from Maya Angelou, Amiri Baraka, Henry Louis Gates, Alice Walker, John Edgar Wideman, Angela Davis, and forty-two other African Americans. Critic Houston A. Baker labeled the letter a "civil action" designed to call attention to a "miscarriage of judgment": "We wanted to call the attention of others to this ignoring of the beauty and greatness of Morrison."

Morrison was stunned by the deluge of support from her peers. On March 31, she was awarded a Pulitzer Prize for *Beloved*, which had been on the bestseller list only eighteen weeks prior to the award. That same cataclysmic year, a list of awards came tumbling after. Fourteen honorary degrees poured in from mostly East Coast institutions, and Morrison was named Tanner Lecturer at the University of Michigan. The attractive, regal, literary matriarch accepted her windfall, winning audiences with her soft-spoken grace and a private, understated sense of self. "It was fabulous," she said. "I loved it. I felt crowned."

In fall 1989, Morrison left her Albany home to accept the Robert F. Goheen Professorship in creative writing, women's studies, and African studies at Princeton, becoming the first black female to be so honored by an Ivy League university.

After receiving the Nobel Prize for literature, Morrison's crowning achievement, she has been besieged by a host of speaking engagements and has been granted honorary memberships in the Center for the Study of Southern Culture, New York Public Library, Helsinki Watch Committee, and advisory council of New York's Queens' College. Despite these new demands, she still struggles to make time for writing as she nurtures new black voices, but she has become an expert at finding privacy and sufficient solitude in order to write. As her father taught her in childhood, she still remains dubious of white society: "I teach my children that there is a part of yourself that you keep from white people—always."

INTRODUCTION TO THE NOVEL

The Bluest Eye, Morrison's first novel, focuses on Pecola (pea-**coal**-uh) Breedlove, a lonely, young black girl living in Ohio in the late 1940s. Through Pecola, Morrison exposes the power and cruelty of white, middle-class American definitions of beauty, for Pecola will be driven mad by her consuming obsession for white skin and blonde hair—and not just blue eyes, but the *bluest* ones. A victim of popular white culture and its pervasive advertising, Pecola believes that people would value her more if she weren't black. If she were white, blonde, and very blue-eyed, she would be loved.

The novel isn't told in a straightforward narrative. In fact, the first paragraph of the novel doesn't seem to be written by Morrison at all; it reads as if it were copied from a first-grade reading book, or primer, one that was used for decades to teach white and black children to read by offering them simple sentences about a picture-perfect, all-American white family composed of Mother, Father, Dick, and Jane.

For those who have never seen this first-grade reading book, go to the library and check out Kismaric and Heiferman's *Growing Up*

With Dick and Jane: Learning and Living the American Dream, published by Collins San Francisco. It contains reproductions of the original Eleanor Campbell watercolor illustrations of squeaky-clean Dick and his blonde-haired, blue-eyed sister Jane, the little girl whom Pecola Breedlove so longs to become.

The second paragraph of the novel contains the same paragraph from the first-grade primer; however, this time, the typography loses all punctuation, a visual metaphor for Pecola's losing her perspective about her worth as a person. Finally, the same paragraph, repeated once more, dissolves into a river of print, having absolutely no meaning, visual evidence of Pecola's consuming madness—a madness that has its genesis in her quest to be beautiful and loved, to have blue eyes, and to experience the happiness and love illustrated in the Mother-Father-Dick-Jane white family.

After this section, Morrison offers us a fragment of memory, set in italics. Claudia MacTeer, a childhood friend of Pecola's, is talking. She says that she remembers the autumn when no marigolds bloomed. That was the fall, she says, when Pecola Breedlove gave birth to her father's baby. *Why* the incest happened, Claudia says, is too difficult to fathom. Perhaps we should be concerned only with *how* it happened: *how* the chaos of Pecola Breedlove's life culminated and climaxed into her giving birth to her own father's child, and then deteriorated into madness.

Morrison divides the rest of the novel into four separate time sequences, each of them a season of the year and each narrated by Claudia MacTeer, now a grown woman. Within these season sequences are narratives by an omniscient, all-knowing voice; these sections are introduced by run-on, unpunctuated lines from the first-grade reading book. Finally, near the end of the novel, a single section records a conversation between Pecola and a fantasy friend that she creates. At last we witness the madness that has enveloped the main character of the novel.

As the novel unfolds, listen to the voices of these two narrators. Remember that Claudia's narration is told in retrospect; she is an adult, looking back. The other narrator, the omniscient narrator, gives us background stories about Pecola's mother and father, as well as seemingly random but interlocking and connecting elements about Pecola's futile longing for blue eyes and her need to feel beautiful and loved in a society that defines her as ugly. In *The Bluest Eye*,

Morrison zeroes in on the psychological damage done to a black girl who self-destructively accepts someone else's definition of beauty—here, the white culture's definition of the ideal way a young girl should look. Pecola's quest is for whiteness, synonymous with beauty; blackness, the symbol for ugliness, is something to be feared and avoided.

LIST OF CHARACTERS

Pecola Breedlove

For the most part, Pecola is a passive, plain young black girl about eleven years old, who is befriended by Claudia and Frieda MacTeer after county officials place her temporarily in their home. During the novel, she suffers the bewildering onset of puberty, bitter racial harassment, and the tragedy of rape and incest.

Claudia MacTeer

One of the novel's narrators; Claudia's childhood memories begin each of the chapters titled Autumn, Winter, Spring, and Summer. Claudia is about nine years old when the events of the novel take place.

Frieda MacTeer

Claudia's older sister, about ten years old. Frieda and Claudia share a childhood friendship with Pecola Breedlove.

Mrs. MacTeer

Claudia and Frieda's mother.

Pauline Breedlove

When she was two years old, she stepped on a rusty nail and afterward walked with a characteristic limp. She is a diligent housekeeper for a wealthy white family and the primary breadwinner for the Breedlove family. She has two children by Cholly Breedlove: Sammy and Pecola.

Cholly Breedlove

When he was four days old, Cholly's mother wrapped him in newspapers and blankets and threw him on a junk heap; his father had already deserted the family. Cholly was raised by his great aunt, called Aunt Jimmy. As an adult, Cholly is frequently drunk, and he is abusive to his wife and children.

Sammy Breedlove

Sammy is the son of Pauline and Cholly Breedlove and the brother of Pecola.

Marie, China, and Poland

Three prostitutes who live in the apartment above the Breedloves; they fascinate Frieda and Claudia, and they befriend Pecola.

Geraldine

A socially conscious, middle-class black woman, Geraldine shows little affection for her son, Louis Junior, but she has enormous adoration for her blue-eyed black cat.

Louis Junior

Geraldine's only child is unloved and deeply troubled; he bullies and torments Pecola.

Elihue Micah Whitcomb (Soaphead Church)

A self-styled spiritualist, "Reader, Advisor, and Interpreter of Dreams," Soaphead's mixed blood keeps him free from the label of being black, although his racial and sexual ambiguities confine him to a life of no identity. Pecola consults him in her quest for blue eyes.

Aunt Jimmy

A kind, generous, earthy woman, she rescues and raises Cholly Breedlove. Oftentimes in the South, an aunt is referred to by her husband's name—for example, Aunt Ed or Aunt Earl; it's possible that Cholly's great aunt was once married to a man named Jimmy.

Blue Jack

Blue befriends a young and impressionable Cholly; because of his storytelling and gentle ways, he becomes a father figure whom Cholly remembers all his life.

Della Jones

Mr. Henry's former landlady; after she suffers a stroke, she seems confused most of the time.

Peggy

A woman from Elyria who is romantically involved with Della Jones' husband.

Old Slack Bessie

Peggy's mother.

Hattie

Della's sister and the object of gossip because of her absent-minded grinning.

Aunt Julia

Della's aunt, known for her eccentricity.

Bay Boy, Woodrow Cain, Buddy Wilson, Junie Bug

A group of black school boys who torment Pecola until she is rescued by Claudia, Frieda, and Maureen Peal.

Dewey Prince

One of Marie's boyfriends.

Rosemary Villanucci

Claudia and Frieda's next-door white neighbor.

Darlene

Cholly Breedlove's first girlfriend; they suffered a humiliating sexual encounter when they were interrupted by jeering white men.

Mr. Henry

A boarder at the MacTeer house; he is beaten by Mr. MacTeer after he touches Frieda's breasts.

Samson Fuller

Cholly Breedlove's father, he abandoned Cholly before the boy was born.

Miss Alice

A close friend of Aunt Jimmy.

M'Dear

A respected midwife, she is known for her knowledge of herbal medicine.

Essie Foster

A neighbor and friend to Cholly and his Aunt Jimmy, her peach cobbler is blamed for causing Aunt Jimmy's death.

O.V.

Aunt Jimmy's half-brother and Cholly's uncle; Cholly doesn't trust him or like him.

Jake

When he is fifteen years old, he meets his cousin Cholly at Aunt Jimmy's funeral; they strike up a friendship and flirt with girls.

Maureen Peal

Claudia and Frieda refer to her as "Meringue Pie"; she is both hated and admired because of her beautiful clothes, light skin, long hair, and green eyes.

Chicken and Pie

Pauline Breedlove's twin siblings, who were under her care before she married Cholly Breedlove.

Mr. and Mrs. Fisher

The well-to-do white couple who employ Pauline as their maid and brag that she is the "ideal servant." They call her "Polly."

Mr. Yacobowski

A fifty-two-year-old white immigrant who owns the neighborhood candy store.

A BRIEF SYNOPSIS

The events in *The Bluest Eye* are not presented chronologically; instead, they are linked by the voices and memories of two narrators. In the sections labeled with the name of a season, Claudia MacTeer's retrospective narration as an adult contains her childhood memories about what happened to Pecola. The other narrator, the omniscient narrator, then braids her stories into Claudia's season sections, introducing influential characters and events that shape Pecola's life.

Claudia MacTeer is now a grown woman, telling us about certain events that happened during the fall of 1941. She was only a child then, but she remembers that no marigolds bloomed that fall, and she and her friends thought it was probably because their friend and playmate, Pecola, was having her father's baby. She tells us that Pecola's father, Cholly Breedlove, is now dead, the baby is dead, and the innocence of the young girls also died that fall.

We then segue into a lengthy flashback, to **Autumn** 1940, a year before the fall when no marigolds bloomed. Claudia and her older sister, Frieda, have just started school. That autumn, the MacTeers accept Mr. Henry as a roomer because his rent money will help pay bills. The family soon has another roomer—Pecola Breedlove, a young black girl whom county officials place in the MacTeer home after Pecola's father burns the family house down.

Pecola and the MacTeer girls share childhood adventures, and what Claudia remembers in particular is the startling onset of Pecola's puberty when the eleven-year-old girl unexpectedly has her first menstrual period.

The second narrator offers us her memories about Pecola's family. She describes the house where the Breedloves lived (before

Cholly burned it down), and she points out the antagonistic relationship between Pecola's parents. We see Pecola and her brother, Sammy, bracing themselves for the ordeal of listening to their mother quarreling violently with their drunken father, Cholly, as he tries to sleep off the effects of the previous night's whiskey.

Against a backdrop of grinding poverty, with her parents locked in an ugly cycle of hostility and violence, Pecola seeks hope in her prayers for beauty, which she feels will lead to her being loved. Each night Pecola fervently prays for blue eyes, sky-blue eyes, thinking that if she looked different—pretty—perhaps everything would be better. Maybe everything would be beautiful.

Claudia's narrative returns with **Winter**. She remembers the arrival of Maureen Peal, a new girl in school, whom Claudia calls "the disrupter." Despite Maureen's protruding dog-tooth and the fact that she was born with an extra finger on each hand (removed at birth), Maureen seems to embody everything perfect; she has long, beautiful hair, light skin, green eyes, and bright, clean, pretty clothes. She is enchanting and popular with both the black and white children.

Pecola is not popular. On the playground, Frieda rescues her from a vicious group of boys who are harassing her. Maureen moves quickly and stands beside Pecola, and the boys leave. Maureen then links arms with Pecola and buys her some ice cream. The world seems wonderful until Maureen begins to talk about Pecola's father's nakedness. Claudia and Frieda quarrel with her, and during the squabble, Claudia swings at Maureen but hits Pecola instead. Maureen runs across the street and screams back at the three girls, "I *am* cute! And you ugly! Black and ugly . . . " Deeply hurt, Pecola curls her shoulders forward in misery.

The omniscient narrator now describes Geraldine, her son Junior, and her much-loved blue-eyed black cat. Neglected by his aloof and status-conscious mother, Junior wickedly lures an unsuspecting Pecola into his house under the pretense of showing her some kittens. Once inside, Junior hurls his mother's big black cat in her face. Scratched and terrified, Pecola moves toward the door, but Junior blocks her way. She is momentarily distracted by the black cat rubbing against her. The blue eyes in the cat's black face mesmerize her.

Junior grabs the cat and begins swinging it in circles. Trying to save the cat, Pecola grabs Junior, who falls and releases the cat, letting it fly full force against the window. Geraldine suddenly arrives home, and Junior immediately blames the cat's death on Pecola.

Claudia's narrative resumes with **Spring**, and she tells us about painful whippings and about her father beating Mr. Henry for touching Frieda's tiny breasts. The sisters go to visit Pecola, who now lives in a drab downstairs apartment; the top floor is home to three prostitutes—Marie ("Miss Maginot Line"), China, and Poland.

The omniscient narrator then tells us about Pauline Breedlove's early life, her marriage to Cholly, the births of Pecola and Sammy, and her job as a servant for a well-to-do white family.

Pauline's story is followed by a recounting of Cholly's traumatic childhood and adolescence. Abandoned by his mother and father, Cholly is raised by a beloved great aunt, Jimmy, who dies when Cholly is a teenager. During Cholly's first sexual experience, he and the girl, Darlene, are discovered by two white men, who mock and humiliate them. Afterward, the pain of humiliation, coupled with the fear that Darlene might be pregnant, prompt Cholly to leave town and head toward Macon, where he hopes to locate his father, Samson Fuller. He finds a belligerent wreck of a man who wants nothing to do with his son. Cholly eventually shakes off the crushing encounter. One day while he is in Kentucky, he meets Pauline Williams, marries her, and fathers two children, Sammy and Pecola.

Years later, on a Saturday afternoon in spring, Cholly staggers home. In a drunken, confused state of love and lust, he rapes eleven-year-old Pecola and leaves her dazed and motionless on the kitchen floor.

The omniscient narrator continues, introducing the character of Elihue Micah Whitcomb, a self-proclaimed psychic and faith healer known as Soaphead Church. He is visited by what he calls a pitifully unattractive black girl of about twelve or so, with a protruding pot belly, who asks him for blue eyes. He tricks her into poisoning a sickly old dog, proclaiming the dog's sudden death as a sign from God that her wish will be granted.

Claudia's narrative returns with **Summer**, and she tells us that she and Frieda learned from gossip that Pecola was pregnant by her father. She remembers the mix of emotions she felt for Pecola—shame, embarrassment, and finally sorrow.

Alone and pregnant, Pecola talks to her only companion—a hallucination. She can no longer go to school, so she wraps herself in a cloak of madness that comforts her into believing that everyone is jealous of her miraculous, new blue eyes.

In this final section, Claudia says that she remembers seeing Pecola after the baby was born prematurely and died. Pecola's brother, Sammy, left town, and Cholly died in a workhouse. Pauline is still doing housework for white folks, and she and Pecola live in a little brown house on the edge of town.

STRUCTURE OF *THE BLUEST EYE*

The following schematic outlines the disparate narrations that make up *The Bluest Eye*. Morrison begins her novel with two fragments resembling a first-grade primer. In each section thereafter, stylistically modified snippets from this fictional primer are interspersed with Claudia's narration, an omniscient narrator's narration, and finally, with Pecola's narration. The outline indicates the placement of these varied texts within the novel's structure.

Fragment 1
Here is the house. (The Dick and Jane primer)

Fragment 2
Quiet as it's kept, there were no marigolds in the fall of 1941. (Claudia)

Autumn
Nuns go by as quiet as lust . . . (Claudia)
HEREISTHEHOUSE . . . There is an abandoned store . . . (narrator)
HEREISTHEFAMILY . . . The Breedloves did not live in a storefront because . . . (narrator)

Winter
My daddy's face is a study. (Claudia)
SEETHECAT . . . They come from Mobile. (narrator)

Spring
The first twigs are thin . . . (Claudia)
SEEMOTHER . . . The easiest thing to do would be to build . . . (narrator and Pauline)
SEEFATHER . . . When Cholly was four days old . . . (narrator)
SEETHEDOG . . . Once there was an old man who loved things . . . (narrator)

Summer
    I have only to break . . . (Claudia)
    LOOKLOOK . . . How many times a minute are you going to look inside . . . ? (Pecola)
    So it was. (Claudia)

CRITICAL COMMENTARIES

Here is the house.

This first fragment seems to be an excerpt from a 1940s American first-grade primer, one that was used for decades to teach white and black students to read. In short, simple sentences, the family in the primer is described as a happy, picture-perfect, American white family, consisting of a big, strong Father, a nice, laughing Mother, a clean-cut son, Dick, and a pretty daughter, Jane.

The paragraph is repeated, and this time all punctuation disappears, along with the capital letters. When the paragraph is repeated a third time, the spacing between the sentences fades, flowing into one long, almost incoherent sentence. The primer's once-perfect sentences are fractured and disjointed, rushing into a flood of words—incomprehensible linguistic chaos.

The perfect world of the happy white family in the first-grade primer is unlike any world Pecola Breedlove knows. In her neighborhood, there are no green and white houses with white doors. In her neighborhood, families are not happy. Jane has a pretty red dress; Pecola does not. Jane's father and mother laugh and play; in Pecola's world, no one laughs or plays, and there are no happy fathers and mothers.

Throughout the novel, excerpts of this primer will be repeated as reminders for readers to be aware of the dichotomy between the black and white cultures. Pecola's tragedy will stem in large part from her unquestionably accepting the image and the values of the white culture; far more than anything else in the primer, she wants to have Jane's blue eyes, fraudulent symbols of real beauty that have no real relationship to lasting happiness and love.

Quiet as it's kept, there were no marigolds in the fall of 1941.

Claudia MacTeer's narration recounts a time in the fall of 1941. Her tone is trusting and warm as she takes us into her confidence.

"Quiet as it's kept" means "Nobody talks about this—it's sort of a secret between *us* . . . " She seems to be confiding to us what was whispered about years ago.

Claudia remembers that no marigolds bloomed that fall, and she and her sister were consumed with worry about the safe delivery of Pecola's baby. In retrospect, nothing came from all their worries and hopes: No flowers bloomed, the baby died, and their innocence was lost forever.

The seeds and earth mentioned in this section are elements of nature that usually symbolize promise and hope, yet here they symbolize barrenness and hopelessness. The season when no marigolds bloomed parallels the deflowering of Pecola, who was raped by her father. His seed withered and died, as did Pecola's hungry soul as it became a mad, barren wasteland.

When Claudia says that Pecola's father dropped his seeds "in his own plot of black dirt," she exposes the very heart of Pecola's anguish. To the white world, Pecola is a "plot of black dirt," inferior because she is black. The figure of speech is darkly ironic, for black dirt is usually the richest of all, but the figurative "black dirt" of Pecola yields nothing.

Autumn

Nuns go by as quiet as lust . . .

Claudia MacTeer, now a grown woman, tells us what happened a year before the fall when no marigolds bloomed. She was nine years old then, sick with a bad cold, and was being nursed through her illness by her mother, whose constant brooding and complaining concealed enormous folds of love and concern for her daughter.

That fall, the MacTeer family—Mrs. MacTeer and her daughters, Frieda and Claudia—stretches to include two new people: Mr. Henry, who moves in after his landlady, Della Jones, becomes incapacitated from a stroke, and Pecola Breedlove, whom the county places in their home after Pecola's father, Cholly, burns down the family house. Pecola's brother moves in with another family, and her mother stays with the white family whom she works for.

Claudia fondly remembers those few days that Pecola stayed with them because she and her sister, Frieda, didn't fight. Mrs. MacTeer fumes and rants, though, when Pecola begins drinking gallon after gallon of milk—simply because the little girl likes to gaze at the golden-haired, blue-eyed, dimple-faced Shirley Temple on the special drinking cup. Claudia also recalls the awe and bewilderment she felt when she witnessed the onset of Pecola's first menstrual period. The girls' reactions range from ignorance and terror as Pecola initially wonders if she is going to die, to Frieda's authoritative reassurances, and finally to Claudia's awe and reverence for the new and different Pecola. Ironically, Pecola is not concerned with her new physical ability to bear children, but with Frieda's assurance that she is now ready to find "somebody . . . to love you." The notion of someone loving her is overwhelming to Pecola; she has never felt loved by anyone.

Using similes and metaphors, Morrison introduces certain characters in this novel by relating them to elements of nature, plants, or animals. For example, black people with property are described as being like "frenzied, desperate birds" in their hunger to own something. Cholly Breedlove is metaphorically described as "an old dog, a snake, a ratty nigger" because he burns the family home and causes his family to be dependent on the kindness of others while he sits in jail. Mr. Henry arrives at the MacTeer home smelling like "trees and lemon vanishing cream." Significantly, Pecola is introduced with no comparisons, no color, no characteristics. She is alone, non-dominating, and devoid of possessions. With no demands of her own, she is easily absorbed into the lives of the other people in the MacTeer house.

As the black characters emerge in Claudia's memories, they are juxtaposed to the characters in the white, perfect world of Dick and Jane and their symbols—in particular, the cute and charming, dimpled face of Shirley Temple on the drinking cup, and the big, white, blue-eyed baby dolls that Claudia has received as presents.

Pecola is so hypnotized by the blue and white Shirley Temple mug, so mesmerized, in fact, that she drinks every ounce of milk in the MacTeer house in an effort to consume this hallmark of American beauty. In contrast, Claudia recalls how she herself reacted when she was given a beautiful white doll to play with, one that had bone-stiff arms, yellow hair, and a pink face. Black adults proclaimed these dolls as beautiful and withheld them from children until they were judged worthy enough to own one. Ironically, when Claudia is finally deemed worthy enough to own one, she dismembers and maims it. She hates it. To her, it is not a thing of beauty.

The Shirley Temple mug that Mrs. MacTeer brings into the house does not have the same mesmerizing effect upon Claudia and Frieda that it does on Pecola; therefore, when they have to stand up to the taunts of the light-skinned Maureen Peal, they can do so. Pecola, however, who has been called ugly so many times—even by her own family—cannot. She doesn't have the emotional stamina to defend or assert herself. Claudia rejects all attempts by others to force feelings of inferiority upon her, but Pecola, lacking the same self-confidence because of her unloving home life, is an easy target for demoralizing propaganda. As a result, she drinks three quarts of milk just to be able to use the Shirley Temple cup and gaze worshipfully at Shirley Temple's blue eyes.

HEREISTHEHOUSE . . . **There is an abandoned store . . .**

This section begins with the madness of words run together, describing a pretty green and white house where two ideal white children, Dick and Jane, play. Dick and Jane are happy and their house is pretty. And then the words *PRETTYPRETTYPRETTYP* suddenly break off, and we are faced with the bleak, colorless, abandoned storefront building where Pecola lives. It stands in startling contrast to the pretty green and white house where the idealized white family lives.

Pecola's house is definitely not pretty; in fact, it is the neighborhood eyesore. The narrator says that it "festers." The building once had life—food was baked here, and gypsy girls occasionally flirted from its open, teasing windows. Now, however, all sense of life has long since drained from it. There is not even a sustained sense of life in the coal stove, which flares and dies erratically.

HEREISTHEFAMILY . . . **The Breedloves did not live in a storefront because . . .**

The excerpt from the first-grade primer talks about Mother and Father, Dick and Jane, the happy white family living in their green and white house. The narrator then introduces the Breedlove family—poor, black, unhappy, and convinced of their ugliness. Father Cholly, a habitual drunk, and Mother Pauline are locked into a violent marriage, while the children, Pecola and Sammy, daily brace themselves to endure their parents' fighting. In this dark world, Pecola prays fervently for blue eyes, believing that if she were pretty and had blue eyes, ugly things wouldn't happen. However, what Pecola doesn't realize is that there are two kinds of ugliness here—real and imagined. The *real* ugliness of one character's words and deeds is juxtaposed to another character's *imagined* ugliness; for example, Maureen's behavior toward Pecola, Claudia, and Frieda could truly be described as "ugly"; on the other hand, Pecola no doubt imagines herself far more uglier than she actually is.

Pecola imagines that she is ugly because of the actions and remarks of people like Mr. Yacobowski, who owns the neighborhood candy store. His unwillingness to touch Pecola's hand is reminiscent of the black dirt metaphor used earlier to describe her. The tension between the two people is taut. Pecola's palms perspire, and for the first time she is aware that she and her body are repulsive to another human being. Morrison emphasizes that the storekeeper does not touch her. Only his nails graze her damp palm, like disembodied claws scratching symbolically at the soft underbelly of a vulnerable target—a little girl's outstretched palm. Once outside the store, utterly convinced of her ugliness, Pecola insatiably consumes Mary Jane candies, staring at the perfect and pretty, blond, blue-eyed girl on the pale wrapper.

Not only Pecola, but everyone in the Breedlove family imagines that they are ugly because they are black; they have accepted the slavemaster's dictum: "You are ugly people." Everything they are familiar with confirms it. Morrison's description has biblical overtones: "And they took the ugliness in their hands, threw it as a mantle over them, and went about the world with it."

All of the Breedloves cope with their "ugliness" differently. Cholly and Sammy *act* ugly, while Pauline escapes into the fantasy world of the movies and her white employer's household. Pecola dreams of blue eyes, a gift that she thinks will suddenly transform her into a thing of beauty; to comfort herself, she snuggles in the warmth of memories and music of the three prostitutes. The phrases "Morning-glory-blue-eyes" and "Alice-and-Jerry-blue-storybook-eyes" comfort her. Later, she will descend into madness in order to rid herself of the ugliness she feels is indelible, and she will embrace a new, imaginary, blue-eyed beautiful self.

(Here and in the following sections, difficult words and phrases are explained.)

- **eating bread and butter** Butter was a treat not often enjoyed by the poor.
- **Black Draught** a liquid, over-the-counter laxative; sometimes it is used to combat colds.
- **Vick's salve** a widely used medication to treat colds; sometimes it is taken internally, although directions on the jar warn against doing so.
- **take holt** a dialectic pronunciation of "take hold of."
- **Alaga syrup** a brand of cough syrup popular in black communities, especially in the South.
- **our roomer** People sometimes rent rooms within their houses (or even apartments) in order to supplement their incomes.
- **Mason jars** glass jars used for canning homegrown fruits and vegetables.
- **Nu Nile Hair Oil** a hair product used by black men.
- **Sen-Sen** a breath freshener made of aromatic dried particles.
- **Greta Garbo** This Swedish-American actress (1905–90) began her career in silent films and successfully switched to "talkies" in the 1930s. Her most famous films include *Mata Hari*, *Anna Karenina*, and *Ninotchka*.
- **Ginger Rogers** Best known for the movie musicals she made as Fred Astaire's dance partner, Rogers (1911–95) received a 1940 Academy Award for best actress for her role in *Kitty Foyle*.
- **Shirley Temple** Adored by everyone, Shirley Temple, with her hallmark dimples, corkscrew golden curls, and twinkling blue eyes, was the highest-paid child actress of the 1930s and early 1940s.
- **Jane Withers** A 1930s-40s tomboy actress with dark eyes and dark hair, she was the antithesis of the Shirley Temple icon.
- **Big Mama and Big Papa** Claudia and Frieda's grandmother and grandfather.
- **Henry Ford** a car manufacturer; one of America's richest men during the 1940s.
- **CCC camps** the Civilian Conservation Corps, a federal jobs program during the 1930s and '40s.
- **ministratin'** a youthful mispronunciation of "menstruating."
- **Lucky Strike** a brand of cigarettes.

- **Chittlin'** here, a nickname; chitterlings, the small intestines of pigs, are a soul food staple—battered, deep-fat fried, and served with lots of catsup, along with corn sticks and cooked greens.

Winter

My daddy's face is a study.

The chapter begins with Claudia's homage to her father, describing him with winter metaphors and similes. His steely, intimidating eyes become a "cliff of snow threatening to avalanche," and "his eyebrows bend like black limbs of leafless trees." Mr. MacTeer is a stark contrast to the previous chapter's description of Cholly Breedlove. MacTeer is a no-nonsense, hard-working man who, like his wife, shows his love for his family more through his deeds than through his words. He works night and day to keep the family safe and financially secure.

In addition to Mr. MacTeer, this section introduces Maureen Peal, a light-skinned black girl who seems to personify enviable white qualities. Maureen is lauded by teachers; Pecola is ignored. Like Jane in the primer, Maureen, the "high-yellow dream child with sloe green eyes," is considered pretty and perfect; in contrast, Pecola is black, flawed, and ugly. Most of Maureen's black schoolmates are blindly enslaved by Maureen's "whiteness"; we know this because of Morrison's description of how Maureen's brown hair is styled: It looks like "two lynch ropes [hanging] down her back." In other words, to worship blindly that which is white is to put your head in a noose.

These black children have been so thoroughly taught to revere whatever is white, or even white-ish, that they are blindly in awe of a black girl who is not even white. She is only "high yellow." Maureen's eyes are not round, blue Anglo eyes; they are described as "sloe," meaning very dark and slanted. In Maureen's case, hers are dark green—certainly not blue. Moreover, Maureen has a "dog tooth," a pointed tooth on the side of the upper jaw, near the front, that has been pushed forward by the teeth on either side growing behind it and toward one another until the dogtooth is prominent, fang-like. In short, Maureen is not really pretty because she has yellowish skin, dark and slanted green eyes, and a fang-like tooth exposed when she smiles. However, being much lighter than all the other black children, she is prized and envied by most of them.

Claudia and her older sister, Frieda, do not adulate Maureen. Claudia relates to her in much the same way that she related to a white baby doll that was given to her one Christmas. At first, she tries to rob Maureen of her power by dismembering her name and calling her "Meringue Pie." Maureen screams at them, "I *am* cute! And you ugly!" and Claudia and Frieda are momentarily stunned before retaliating with a full arsenal of insults.

The black boys who torment Pecola do so because of their lack of self-worth. They see their own blackness and their own ugliness in Pecola. Because they have been successfully brainwashed by ubiquitous and subtle pro-white propaganda to despise all that is black, they set upon Pecola as if they were trying to exorcise their own blackness.

References to the icons of Hollywood's white standards of beauty abound: Betty Grable's appearing at the Dreamland Theater is mentioned, and Hedy Lamarr's name is casually thrown into a conversation when Maureen insults black females who would dare to request a hairstyle like Hedy Lamarr's when they know they'll never have hair like that. Mr. Henry uses the names of Ginger Rogers and Greta Garbo as pet names for Claudia and Frieda, as if being called by the names of these famous white beauties would be perceived as a great compliment.

In addition to the all-pervasive white notion of what constitutes beauty, we hear about adult deception in this chapter. Both Claudia and Frieda are disappointed in Mr. Henry when he demonstrates that adults lie to children. First, he tricks them into leaving the house by giving them money for candy. Upon their unexpected and hasty return, he lies about his female guests, telling the children that the prostitutes are really members of his Bible reading class. The girls must then pretend that they believe Mr. Henry's absurd explanation. We see that children are far more perceptive than adults believe them to be.

SEETHECAT . . . **They come from Mobile.**

This section of the novel begins with an excerpt from the primer that contains a reference to the soft, cuddly orange kitten that lives with the ideal white family. The story that follows, however, is far from ideal. Geraldine, a prim and proper middle-class black woman, is obsessed with distinguishing herself and her family from lower-class blacks, which leads her to inadvertently abuse her family emotionally.

Mother Geraldine, Father Louis, and son Junior epitomize the black middle class, which has become far distanced from its black roots. Geraldine consciously removes herself from, and looks down on, black people who do not have white middle-class aspirations. According to Morrison, Geraldine is one of those blacks who "when they wear lipstick . . . never cover the entire mouth for fear of lips too thick . . . " Geraldine is obsessed with white "things": a manicured lawn, an overly decorated house, straightened hair, and a silent communal vow to banish anything lustful, lively, or passionate from her life. Her quest for upward social mobility encompasses a self-hatred that makes her avoid all reminders of her African heritage.

Geraldine measures out her emotions: Her son, Junior, is bathed and slathered with white lotion, and her husband, Louis, is granted a finite amount of sex, as long as he doesn't touch her too much. Only the blue-eyed black cat kindles any real affection within her. Thus Junior develops a malignant jealousy, a cruel sibling rivalry toward the cat. Not allowed to play with blacks, and not accepted by whites, he has learned to vent his frustration by bullying young girls and abusing his mother's blue-eyed black cat.

On a rare day when Geraldine is out of the house, Junior spies Pecola walking alone and invites her in to see some kittens. Once she is inside the house, he hurls his mother's black cat in her face. Scratched and terrified, Pecola turns to leave, but Junior blocks the door, grabs the cat, and begins to swing it in circles. As Pecola tries to save the cat, she falls on Junior, who lets go of the cat, flinging it against the window. Geraldine arrives home, and Junior blames the cat's death on Pecola.

Geraldine is afraid and repulsed by Pecola's presence in her house. Her precious and perfect house has been invaded by a creature with matted hair and a dirty, torn dress. Pecola represents everything that Geraldine despises—disorder, black poverty, and filthy ugliness. Pecola's humiliation takes place in the pretty house with the pretty lady's grisly words—"nasty little black bitch"— filtered through the fur of the dead, blue-eyed black cat. The last image Pecola sees as she is absorbed into the cold March wind is the sad and unsurprised gaze of Jesus, the same Jesus whom she prays to every night, begging for blue eyes.

- ***Imitation of Life*** a black-and-white film released in 1934, in which a white woman becomes rich through the pancake recipe of her black servant; meantime, the black servant is deeply saddened when her light-skinned daughter chooses to pass for white. This version of the Fannie Hurst novel starred Claudette Colbert.
- **Claudette Colbert** An American stage and film actress (1903–96) born in Paris, she won an Academy Award for best actress in *It Happened One Night*.
- **Betty Grable** An American actress and film star (1916–73), she was the most popular pin-up girl of World War II; she co-starred with Ginger Rogers and Fred Astaire in *The Gay Divorcee* (1934) and later appeared in such films as *Moon Over Miami* (1941) and *The Pin-Up Girl* (1944).
- **Hedy Lamarr** An American film actress born Hedwig Kiesler in Vienna, Austria (1913–), she co-starred with Judy Garland in *Ziegfield Girl* (1941) and later starred in Cecil B. DeMille's *Samson and Delilah* (1949).
- **Maginot Line** a system of heavy fortifications built before World War II on the eastern frontier of France; it failed to prevent invasion by the Nazi forces.
- **Shet up!** a dialectic pronunciation of "Shut up!"
- **incorrigival** a youthful mispronunciation of "incorrigible," unable to be corrected, improved, or reformed.

Spring

The first twigs are thin . . .

Claudia recalls spring, and her memories sting, for whenever she was punished that spring, she was always whipped with fresh forsythia twigs that bent but never broke. Spring is a season often associated with sexuality, and Claudia remembers she and her sister being introduced ever more dramatically to the disturbing and deceptive world of adult sexuality. In an earlier episode, Mr. Henry, whom the girls trusted and adored, deceived them when he entertained prostitutes in their house. Now he touches Frieda's budding breasts, and Mr. MacTeer tries to kill him because Frieda might be "ruined," an adult term used to describe a girl or woman who has lost her virginity. The word is confusing to the girls; Mrs. MacTeer has used it to describe the prostitutes, and Claudia has mistakenly assumed it means "fat."

Seeking liquor, which the girls mistakenly believe will "eat up" fat, they go looking for Pecola, reasoning, "Her father's always drunk. She can get us some." They find her, far away on Lake Shore Park, where her mother, Pauline, works for a white family named Fisher. There, they witness Pauline unleashing a lifelong fury of hatred upon her daughter after Pecola accidentally drops a pan containing blueberry cobbler, burning her little legs severely. The girls are troubled when Pauline, who is bitter and rough with her own daughter, is loving and comforting with the Fishers' daughter. They know it is Pauline's own child who needs comforting most. In this scene, note that whereas Pecola calls her mother "Mrs. Breedlove," the little Fisher girl, assuming a superior attitude toward an adult servant of the family, condescendingly calls Pecola's mother "Polly."

SEEMOTHER . . . The easiest thing to do would be to build . . .

This section begins with an excerpt from the first-grade primer about the picture-perfect white Mother. The white Mother is very nice; she plays and sings. She is not like Pauline Breedlove, the black mother whom we saw mercilessly abusing her daughter because of an accident. How did Pauline come to be the mother who disciplines her daughter so harshly? Morrison explains it this way: When Pauline was two years old, she stepped on a nail, and ever afterward that foot flopped, making her feel separated from other people and unworthy.

A quiet, private girl, Pauline was responsible for her two young twin siblings, Chicken and Pie, while her mother worked. She enjoyed keeping house, arranging and straightening things, and being neat and meticulous. She dreamed of meeting a good-looking, loving man, and when she did, she and Cholly Breedlove moved to Lorain, Ohio, where he worked in a steel mill. Having little to do, Pauline began going to the movies, where she filled her life with fantasy.

Laced into the narrative of this chapter are letter-like memories, seemingly spoken or written by Pauline about her life with Cholly—how it changed, how she changed. She remembers Cholly as a strapping man with his own music, who, in contrast to everyone else, touched her broken foot and kissed her leg. Cholly was her rainbow man. During the early years of their marriage, Pauline's sexual orgasms were multicolored. She describes how she felt herself becoming the deep purple of ripe berries, the cool yellow of lemonade, flowing with streaks of green, and how all the colors coalesced when Cholly touched her. Pauline describes the feeling as being like "laughing between my legs." Years later, there is no laughter and no rainbows. Pauline is living in a cold, gray, lifeless building; Cholly has turned to liquor, and Pauline has again turned to fantasy. Earlier, she soothed her troubled soul in the promises of church hymns, and then in the fairy-tale world of the movies. Now she finds happiness in the beautiful, fantasy-like world of the white, affluent Fisher family, where there is an abundance of virtue, beauty, and order.

SEEFATHER . . . When Cholly was four days old . . .

The father in the first-grade primer is physically strong; so is Cholly Breedlove—and there the similarities end. The primer asks of the white father: Will you play with Jane? We suppose he does; he is a loving, doting father. Cholly Breedlove, however, doesn't play with his daughter; instead, he rapes her during one of his drunken binges. And later, he rapes her again.

What drives a man to rape his own daughter? Of all the hard luck stories we've encountered so far in this novel, nothing can equal Cholly's story—especially his early years, when he was abandoned by his father before he was born, then wrapped in newspapers and thrown on a junk heap by his mother after he was born. Mentored by Blue Jack, an old drayman, and raised for a while by an old great aunt, Aunt Jimmy, Cholly was basically rootless for most of his life. After he and a young girl, Darlene, are caught having sex by a couple of derisive white men, Cholly strikes out on his own. Darlene may be pregnant, but Cholly isn't anxious to assume the role of a responsible father, and, more important, he feels the need to find his own father. Ironically, he is willing to abandon the child that Darlene may be carrying in order to find the father who abandoned him.

When he is angrily rejected by Samson Fuller, fourteen-year-old Cholly's resolve shatters, and he flees outside and soils himself with bowels that have needed to be relieved since he boarded the bus in Macon, Georgia.

After Cholly is metaphorically cleansed in a river, he takes charge of his life, feeling free to do whatever he wants—satisfy his lust with prostitutes, sleep in doorways, work thirty days on a chain gang, do odd jobs and leave them spontaneously, spend time in jail without resenting it, kill three white men, knock a woman in the head if he wants to, or be gentle if he chooses to be. For the first time in his life, Cholly feels free; in Morrison's words, he feels "godlike."

It is in this godlike frame of mind that Cholly meets Pauline Williams, marries her, and produces two children, Sammy and Pecola. However, without any understanding of how to raise children, having never known a healthy parent-child relationship or even enjoyed the basic security of parental affection, Cholly reacts to all family problems according to the mood he's in, never considering the emotional needs of his wife or small children.

The tangled sequence surrounding Pecola's rape exposes Cholly's painful memories of his humiliating sexual experience with Darlene, the passion he felt for Pauline years ago, and the forbidden desire he has for Pecola—despite his initial repulsion for her small, ugly, humped body, bending over the dish pan as he approaches her. In his drunkenness, Cholly confuses his long-ago feelings for Pauline with his attraction to his emotionally fractured daughter, standing at the sink, one foot scratching her leg, the same way Pauline was doing the first time he saw her in Kentucky. Drunkenly, he equates his forced physical contact with Pecola as an act of love because she loves him so unconditionally and because he knows he doesn't deserve her love. Afterward, he looks at Pecola and is filled with revulsion, the same feeling he felt for Darlene. However, before he leaves her, he covers her tenderly with a quilt, a meager gesture which in no way compensates for his violent transgression.

SEETHEDOG . . . Once there was an old man who loved things . . .

The description of the mangy dog that torments Soaphead Church in this chapter contrasts markedly with the description of the dog that belongs to the picture-perfect white family in the first-grade primer. The old dog, whose weary carcass vexes Soaphead, is the antithesis of the primer's playful, perky dog.

Elihue Micah Whitcomb, known as Soaphead Church, is nauseated by the sickly old dog, just as he is nauseated by most people. Yet he is comfortable with the realization that he is a misanthrope, for he realized his disdain for people at an early age. Paradoxically, however, he has dabbled in professions that have placed him squarely in their midst. For a time, he was an Anglican priest, then a social caseworker, and now he is a "Reader, Advisor, and Interpreter of Dreams," a career choice that promises him a little money while guaranteeing him a minimal amount of close contact with people.

Reared in a family that believed their academic and intellectual achievements were based on their mixed blood, Soaphead Church cultivated habits and tastes that separated him from all things African. His skills in language and self-deception have allowed him to palm himself off as a minister and faith healer. People come to him asking for basic needs: love, health, and money.

Pecola Breedlove, however, has a unique request: blue eyes. Surprisingly, her request is logical to Soaphead. To him, she's a "pitifully unattractive" child, and blue eyes would definitely be an improvement. He feels sorry for Pecola, but not because of the recognition of his exploitative profession; rather, his pity is borne out of the impotence of not being able to give her blue eyes, which he believes she should have in order to be beautiful. Soaphead is not sorry that she has been brainwashed into thinking she's ugly; he is simply sorry that Pecola is indeed an ugly child and is doomed to eternal ugliness because of her coarse African features. His pity for her, however, does not preclude his seizing this opportunity to rid himself of his landlord's mangy dog. Thus he tells her that she must make an offering to God, handing her a piece of rancid raw meat, on which (unbeknownst to Pecola) he has sprinkled poison. He tells her to feed the meat to the mangy dog on the porch. If nothing happens to the dog, God will not give her blue eyes. If the dog behaves strangely, however, God will give her blue eyes the next day.

At this point, we have met Maureen Peal, Geraldine, and now Elihue Micah Whitcomb, three examples of blacks who make it their life's work to deny their blackness. All of them have found Pecola ugly, and all of them have victimized her because of her strong African features. Pecola is not alone in equating black features with the word "ugly"; everyone, with the exception of Claudia and her older sister, Frieda, seems to feel the same way. Thus we have Morrison's blanket condemnation of white society's insistence that only white features are acceptable and pretty, and for black America's endorsement of that fraud.

- **Fels Naphtha**   a popular cleaning product.
- **dicty-like**   black slang for snobbish, or haughty.
- **Clark Gable**   an American film actor (1901–60) who personified his era's notion of the virile, adventurous American male. He won an Academy Award for *It Happened One Night* (1934) and is best known for his portrayal of Rhett Butler in *Gone With the Wind* (1939).
- **Jean Harlow**   Hollywood's prototype for the American blonde bombshell, Harlow (1911–37) went on to reign supreme in the films of the early 1930s and starred opposite Clark Gable in *Red Dust* (1932) and *China Seas* (1935).
- **drays**   low, sturdily built carts with detachable sides for carrying oversize loads.
- **muscadine**   a musky grape grown in the southeast United States; often used for making wine.
- **gandy dancers**   workers on a railroad section gang; they are probably named because of the movements made while using tools from the Gandy Manufacturing Company.
- **asafetida bags**   small bags often used in folk medicine, filled with a bitter, foul-smelling mixture from the roots of various Asiatic plants, and worn around the neck in order to ward off disease.
- **slop jar**   an indoor container that takes the place of toilets, especially for night use or for people too ill to walk outside to an outhouse.
- **Anglophile**   a term applied to someone who has an enormous admiration for and devotion to things British.
- **De Gobineau**   a French diplomat and social philosopher (1816–82) whose racial theories became a philosophical justification for Nazi "ethnic cleansing." His most famous work, *Essay on the Inequality of Human Races*, states that the Aryan race is superior to all other races. His theory of racial superiority has been thoroughly refuted, of course, and is considered worthless by modern anthropologists.
- **met his Beatrice**   Beatrice (pronounced Bay-ah-**tree**-chay) was the ideal woman, beloved by the poet Dante and the symbol of divine and ideal love. She leads Dante through one portion of the *Divine Comedy*.

- **sealing wax**   a combination of resin and turpentine that is used for sealing letters.
- **misanthrope**   a person who hates and distrusts people.
- **pomaded with soap lather**   using soap lather as a hair-grooming product.
- **Hamlet's abuse of Ophelia**   Ophelia is in love with Hamlet, who treats her with alternating contempt and tenderness. She is a tragic character, driven mad by unrequited love, and drowns herself after Hamlet mistakenly kills her father.
- **Christ's love of Mary Magdalene**   According to the Gospels, Mary of Magdala was cured of seven demons by Christ (Luke 8:2) and was at the foot of the cross when he was crucified (Mark 15:40). According to popular tradition, Mary Magdalene was also the woman who, on two occasions (Luke 7:37-38 and John 12:3), washed and anointed Jesus' feet, drying them with her hair. She has become symbolic of repentant sinners.
- **Gibbon**   Edward Gibbon (1737-94) is best known for his six-volume *History of the Decline and Fall of the Roman Empire*. In this work, which covers a time span of thirteen centuries, Gibbon espoused the view that the decline and fall were inevitable because of the withering of the classical tradition of intellectual inquiry. He blamed this trend, in part, on the rise of Christianity. His negative treatment of Christianity and his bitter irony made the work a subject of controversy.
- **Othello, Desdemona, Iago**   characters from Shakespeare's *Othello*. Othello the dark Moor marries the fair, blonde Desdemona and is deceived by the villainous Iago, who falsely accuses Desdemona of being unfaithful. In a fit of jealousy, Othello kills her.
- **Dante**   an Italian poet (1265-1321) best known for his *Divine Comedy*, which details his vision as he progresses through Hell and Purgatory, escorted by the poet Virgil, and is guided to Paradise by his lifelong idealized love, Beatrice, who leads him to the throne of God.
- **Dostoevsky**   a Russian writer (1821-81) whose works combine religious mysticism with profound psychological insight. He is best known for his *Crime and Punishment* and *The Brothers Karamazov*.
- **Greater and Lesser Antilles**   The whole of the West Indies, except the Bahamas, is called the Antilles. The Greater Antilles include Cuba, Jamaica, Haiti, the Dominican Republic, and Puerto Rico. The Lesser Antilles include the Virgin Islands, Windward Islands, Leeward Islands, the southern group of the Netherlands Antilles, Barbados, Trinidad, and Tobago.

Summer

I have only to break . . .

Claudia recounts some of the things she associates with one particular summer: strawberries, sudden thunderstorms, and gossip about her friend Pecola. Through fragments of gossip, Claudia and Frieda learn that Pecola is pregnant and that the baby's father is Pecola's own father. According to gossip, only a miracle can save the baby.

Claudia and Frieda believe they must do more than just pray for the health and safe delivery of Pecola's baby because it will be the antithesis of the white baby dolls that Claudia has always despised. However, a miracle of this magnitude requires that they sacrifice their money and bury it near Pecola's house, sacrifice their dreams of a new bicycle, promise God they will be good for a whole month, and plant marigold seeds in the backyard. When the seeds come up, the girls will know that everything is all right.

Claudia and Frieda want Pecola's baby to live in order to validate their own blackness and to counteract the universal love for white baby dolls, Shirley Temple look-alikes, and the black community's flawed-but-Anglicized beauty, Maureen Peel. The principle they want to reverse is the so-called mulatto aesthetic, which dictates that those blacks who are considered the most beautiful are those who most closely resemble whites. Throughout their own black community, the two girls hear whisperings about Pecola's "ugliness," Cholly's "ugliness," and the seemingly inevitable, monstrous "ugliness" of Pecola's baby. The key word here, of course, is "ugly," a word describing anyone who has pronounced black facial features that Morrison describes as a head covered with great O's of wool, two clean black eyes like nickels, a flared nose, kissing-thick lips, "and the living, breathing silk of black skin"—all positive, beautiful, admirable features.

LOOKLOOK . . . How many times a minute are you going to look inside . . . ?

This frenzied primer excerpt introduces a friend who will play with Jane, the fictional picture-perfect white girl. Pecola has a "friend," too, but hers is not real. It is a hallucination. Pecola's schizophrenia has created an imaginary friend for her because she has no real friends—Claudia and Frieda now avoid her. Not even her mother is a friend. Pauline Breedlove didn't believe that Pecola was an innocent victim of Cholly's drunken rape. She blamed Pecola, and that is why Pecola never told her mother about the second rape; Pauline wouldn't have believed that her daughter was an innocent victim in that incident either.

Alone, with no one to turn to, Pecola creates her own imaginary friend, someone who will listen while she talks about her new blue eyes. Everyone, we hear, is jealous of how pretty and "really, truly, bluely nice" they are, so perfect and powerful that not even strong sunlight can force Pecola to blink. She believes they're such blindingly blue eyes that people have to look away when they see her, but the real reason people avoid her, of course, concerns the stigma of incest. Her fantasizing that she now has blue eyes compensates for the nightmare memory of the horrible episode in the kitchen when Cholly forced himself on her, as well as the second time, when she was reading on the couch.

And yet, there's a chance that someone, somewhere, somehow, *may* have bluer eyes. That possibility bothers Pecola because she wants to have the bluest eyes of all.

Pecola has drowned in madness. She has been destroyed by a cultural perversion that wholly negates the dreams and aspirations of black-skinned, brown-eyed people (girls, in particular) who do not measure up to the blonde, blue-eyed American myth. Because this prejudice is so universal, it often affects even whites who might be considered unattractive by their own Anglican standards if they aren't sufficiently blond or blue-eyed.

So it was.

The time is the present. Claudia tells us that Sammy Breedlove left town, Cholly died in a workhouse, and Mrs. Breedlove is still doing housework for whites. She herself has attempted to understand her role in Pecola's tragedy because the destruction to Pecola was absolute and complete. The baby was born prematurely and died. Afterward, Pecola's bizarre and erratic behavior forced people either to look away or laugh out loud; Claudia and Frieda simply avoided her. Earlier, Pecola's passive ability to be wounded allowed Maureen to gloat with superiority and allowed Geraldine to hiss, "You nasty little black bitch." Mr. Yacobowski's "glazed separateness" placed Pecola outside of the realm of human recognition, and even the bizarre Soaphead Church saw her as an ugly little black curio whom he could use. Claudia's revelation that Cholly was the only one who loved Pecola enough to touch her underscores that he alone—even in his own violent, perverted way—understood the agony of the fixed, penetrating presence of the untouchable and intrusive white society. The devastating power of racial contempt and self-hatred has caused Pecola, a mere child, to literally self-destruct in her quest for love, self-worth, and identity.

- **Moirai** In classical Greek mythology, they are the Fates, the goddesses of birth and death.

CHARACTER ANALYSES

PECOLA BREEDLOVE

Pecola is the eleven-year-old black girl around whom the story revolves. She is abused by almost everyone in the novel and eventually suffers two traumatic rapes. Pecola's experiences, however, are not typical of all black girls who also have to grow up in a hostile society.

Except for Claudia and Frieda, Pecola has no friends. She is ridiculed by most of the other children and is insulted and tormented by black schoolboys because of her dark skin and coarse features. She realizes that no one—except Claudia and Frieda—will play with her, socialize with her, or be seen with her. She is raped by her drunken father and self-deceived into believing that God has miraculously given her the blue eyes that she prayed for. She loses her baby, and shortly afterward she loses her sanity.

All little black girls try to grow up into healthy women with positive self-images—despite the fact that white society seems to value and love only little girls with blue eyes, yellow hair, and pink skin. Today, most black girls survive the onslaught of white media messages, but even today, some fail. Pecola, a little black girl in the 1940s, does not survive. She is the "broken-winged bird that cannot fly."

Tormented and even tortured by almost everyone with whom she comes into contact, Pecola never fights back. If she had had the inner strength of Claudia and Frieda, she would have been able to counter the meanness of others toward her by assuming a meanness of her own. She does not. She is always the victim, always the object of others' wrath. Pauline abuses Pecola when she accidentally spills the cobbler all over the floor of the Fishers' kitchen, Junior tricks her into his house for the sole purpose of tormenting her, Geraldine hurts Pecola's feelings when she throws Pecola out of her house and calls her "black," as if to insult her, and Mr. Yacobowski degrades her by refusing to touch her hand to take her money. The schoolboys torment Pecola about her ugly blackness, Maureen buys her an ice cream cone in order to "get into her business," and she is psychologically abused by the degrading conditions under which she and her brother, Sammy, live as they watch their parents abuse one another.

Pecola has never had proper clothing or food, and she is eventually put out of her own home because her father starts a fire in one of his drunken stupors and burns down the house. Soaphead Church uses her to kill a dog that he doesn't have the courage or resolve to kill himself. Cholly abuses Pecola in the most dramatically obscene way possible—and never once does Pecola fight back. She might have yelled back at the boys who tormented her after school the way Frieda did; she might have thrown her money at Mr. Yacobowski when he refused to touch her hand; she might have started a fight with Maureen when Maureen began questioning her about her father's nakedness. Had Pecola taken the ugliness that society defined for her and turned it outward, she would not have become society's victim.

CLAUDIA AND FRIEDA MACTEER

One of the narrators of the novel, Claudia remembers the events of one year in her childhood that culminated in the rape and madness of an eleven-year-old friend, Pecola Breedlove. Growing up in a black, nurturing, functional—albeit poor—family, Claudia is Pecola's opposite. Her negative and even violent reaction to white dolls lets us know that she has the ability to survive in an inverted world order that would teach her to despise herself. Although the stiff-limbed, blue-eyed, yellow-haired, pink-skinned dolls are lovingly given to her at Christmas, Claudia resents them and dismembers them.

Claudia recognizes her own inner worth—as well as her own inner violence. She enjoys destroying the white dolls because as she does so, she is satisfying her resentment of white girls and white values that would label her as black and ugly.

Claudia and her older sister, Frieda, have learned their life lessons from their mother. They have learned how to be strong black females who can fight back and not be overwhelmed and brainwashed by standards of beauty imposed on them by white *and* black women.

Even when Mrs. MacTeer is singing the blues and fussing at her daughters, there is love throughout their house; in contrast, there is no love in Pecola's house. Because of their mother's strengths and examples, both Claudia and Frieda are able to fight back against the forces that threaten to destroy them psychologically. Both girls resent the fact that not only white society but also black society values the Maureen Peals of the world. They realize that they must create their own self-worth in this world of beauty to which they don't belong.

PAULINE

A woman of many contradictions, Pauline resists the Anglo brainwashing in her early years; she doesn't straighten her hair or wear makeup. However, she begins secretly to enjoy her movie star fantasies and the multicolored rainbow orgasms when she makes love with Cholly. After she has been fired by a white employer and treated like an animal by white doctors, she begins perversely to treat her daughter, Pecola, with the same contempt. She is often cruel, cold, and aloof to Pecola as she looks at her daughter's eyes and sees only ugliness.

Saddled with an alcoholic husband, a rootless son, and an ugly daughter, Pauline turns to a picture-perfect white family for happiness and fulfillment. Transforming herself into the white family's "perfect servant," she becomes Polly, parroting the Fishers' white attitudes and even consoling the little pink-and-white Fisher girl at the expense of her own confused and injured daughter's feelings.

CHOLLY BREEDLOVE

To Cholly, being a parent means to abuse and to desert. His parents did both to him. Raised for a short time by a caring great aunt and sustained for a while by the kindness of Blue Jack, a fatherly stand-in, Cholly grows to adulthood never knowing the sustained, protective, unconditional love of family members.

Cholly defines himself as a "free man" because not only does he function on the periphery of society as other blacks are expected to, but he also lives outside the society of the black community and is the constant source of their gossip. He is responsible for the destruction of his family's home through a fire that he carelessly starts, yet he doesn't care that the community looks down on him for this act.

Cholly fights with his wife in front of his children, neglects his family for his social life, and doesn't provide even the barest of necessities for them. He is the despicable absentee father, an outcast in his own home. As a father, he is the antithesis of Dick and Jane's flawless white father. He abuses his wife, Pauline, then deserts her as he retreats into a world of alcoholic chaos. In a confused state of love and lust, fueled by drunkenness, he rapes his daughter, Pecola, and leaves her on the kitchen floor.

Eventually he dies in a workhouse.

SOAPHEAD CHURCH (ELIHUE MICAH WHITCOMB)

Proud of the intermingling of the races that produced him, Soaphead Church, a self-proclaimed Anglophile, is so pleased with his looks that he is initially revolted by Pecola's appearance. Later, however, her dark skin, kinky hair, and poverty-stricken appearance turn his revulsion into pity: Although some people are able to rise above their defects, he knows instinctively that Pecola will never do so. He senses a doomed quality about her.

Misanthropic in his perversity, Soaphead is reviled by human contact. He is nauseated by the "humanness" of people—their body odor, breath odor, blood, sweat, tears, decayed or missing teeth, ear wax, blackheads, moles, blisters, skin crusts—all of the body's survivalist protections.

Mixed blood and white ancestry were always important to Soaphead's family, the Whitcombs—more important, in fact, than how the family was actually treated by their white, reluctant relatives. To the Whitcombs, whites were always superior and therefore beautiful; as a result, they cherished their relationship with whites and sought to maintain their heritage of light skin.

Because the thought of being near a woman is abhorrent to Soaphead, he has begun to prefer the company of young girls. His effete and fastidious mannerisms detract from whatever masculinity he might have developed. Not surprisingly, his eccentricities alienate him from most people, which pleases him.

CRITICAL ESSAY

AN OVERVIEW OF *THE BLUEST EYE*

Morrison's story about a young black girl's growing self-hatred begins with an excerpt from a typical first-grade primer from years ago. The tone is set immediately: "Good" means being a member of a happy, well-to-do white family, a standard that is continually juxtaposed against "bad," which means being black, flawed, and strapped for money. If one is to believe the first-grade primer, everyone is happy, well-to-do, good-looking, and white. One would never know that black people existed in this country. Against this laughing, playing, happy white background, Morrison juxtaposes the novel's black characters, and she shows how all of them have been affected in some way by the white media—its movies, its books, its myths, and its advertising. For the most part, the blacks in this novel have blindly accepted white domination and have therefore given expensive white dolls to their black daughters at Christmas. Mr. Henry believes that he is being complimentary when he calls Frieda and Claudia "Greta Garbo" and "Ginger Rogers." The schoolchildren—the black schoolboys, in particular—are mesmerized by the white-ish Maureen Peal, and Maureen herself enjoys telling about the black girl who dared to request a Hedy Lamarr hairstyle.

The Bluest Eye is a harsh warning about the old consciousness of black folks' attempts to emulate the slave master. Pecola's request is not for more money or a better house or even for more sensible parents; her request is for blue eyes—something that, even if she had been able to acquire them, would not have abated the harshness of her abject reality.

Pecola's story is very much her own, unique and dead-end, but it is still relevant to centuries of cultural mutilation of black people in America. Morrison does not have to retell the story of three hundred years of black dominance by white culture for us to be aware of the history of American blacks, who have been victims in this tragedy.

The self-hatred that is at the core of Pecola's character affects, in one degree or another, all of the other characters in the novel. As noted earlier, a three-hundred-year-old history of people brought to the United States during the period of slavery has led to a psychological oppression that fosters a love of everything connected with the slave masters, while promoting a revulsion toward everything connected with themselves. All cultures teach their own standards of beauty and desirability through billboards, movies, books, dolls, and other products. The white standard of beauty is pervasive throughout this novel—because there is no black standard of beauty.

Standing midway between the white and black worlds is the exotic Maureen Peal, whose braids are described as "two lynch ropes." Morrison's chilling description of Maureen's hair is intentional, for she is referring to the young black men who look in awe at the white-ish Maureen. These young men, she is saying, are symbolic of all of the black men who have allowed themselves to be mesmerized by Anglo standards of beauty. As a result, they turn on their own—just as the boys turn on Pecola. Her blackness forces the boys to face their own blackness, and thus they make Pecola the scapegoat for their own ignorance, for their own self-hatred, and for their own feelings of hopelessness. Pecola becomes the dumping ground for the black community's fears and feelings of unworthiness.

From the day she is born, Pecola is told that she is ugly. Like many other blacks, Pecola's mother, Pauline, is more concerned with the appearance of her new baby than she is with its health. Pecola learns from her mother that she is ugly, and she thereby learns to hate herself; because of her blackness, she is continually bombarded by rejection and humiliation from others around her who value "appearance."

Unfortunately, Pecola does not have the sophistication to realize that she is not the only little black girl who doesn't have the admired, valued Anglo features—neither do most of the blacks who torment her. Pecola knows only that she wants to be prized and loved, and she believes that if she could look white, she would be loved. However, she becomes the scapegoat for all of the other black characters, for, in varying degrees, they too suffer from the insanity that manifests itself in Pecola's madness.

If Morrison seems to focus on female self-hatred in Pecola, it is clear that feelings of self-hatred are not limited to black girls alone.

Boys receive just as much negative feedback from the white community, but they are far more likely to direct their emotions and retaliation outward, inflicting pain on others before the pain turns inward and destroys them. Cholly and Junior are prime examples.

After the publication of *The Bluest Eye*, Morrison explained that she was trying to show the nature and relationship between parental love and violence. One of the novel's themes is that parents, black parents in this case, do violence to their children every day—if only by forcing them to judge themselves by white standards. The topic of child abuse, once a socially unmentionable subject, remained unaddressed far too long, even though everyone knew about it. Mr. Henry's touching Frieda's breasts is a subtle preparation, or foreshadowing, of Cholly Breedlove's rape of Pecola. When Cholly rapes Pecola, it is a physical manifestation of the social, psychological, and personal violence that has raped Cholly for years. His name is "Breedlove" but he is incapable of loving; he is only able to perform the act of breeding. Because he has been so depreciated by white society, he is reduced to breeding with his own daughter, a union so debased that it produces a stillborn child, one who cannot survive for even an hour in this world where self-hatred breeds still more self-hatred.

REVIEW QUESTIONS AND ESSAY TOPICS

(1) Discuss the narrative structure of the novel. Why might Morrison have chosen to present the events in a non-chronological way?

(2) Write an essay in which you discuss Morrison's juxtaposing the primer's Mother-Father-Dick-Jane sections with Claudia's and the omniscient narrator's sections. What is the relationship between these three differing narrative voices?

(3) Discuss the significance of no marigolds blooming in the fall of 1941.

(4) Compare Pecola's character to Claudia's. Which of these two characters is better able to reject white, middle-class America's definitions of beauty? Support your answer with examples from the text.

(5) Discuss the symbolism associated with Shirley Temple in the novel. What does she represent to Pecola? What might she represent to Maureen Peal?

(6) Discuss Cholly's dysfunctional childhood. What is his definition of what a family should be? Does knowing about his upbringing affect your reactions when he rapes Pecola? Why or why not?

(7) How does Morrison present gender relations in the novel? Are men and women's relationships generally portrayed positively or negatively? Support your answer with examples from the text.

(8) Write an essay in which you compare Louis Junior's and Soaphead Church's treatment of Pecola. Is she treated worse by one of these characters than the other? If so, which one, and why? Is it significant that each relationship involves animals?

(9) Discuss the mother-daughter relationships in the novel.

(10) Does Morrison present any positive role models for Pecola and other girls like her? How might Morrison define what beauty is? Does she present any examples of such beauty in the novel?

(11) Write an essay in which you discuss Pecola's dream of happiness and Langston Hughes' poem "Dream Deferred." Is Pecola's wanting the bluest eyes a "dream deferred"? Discuss Pecola's dream in terms of its worth, compared to the dreams of young Pauline, the dreams of Louis Junior's mother, Geraldine, and the dreams of Soaphead Church. What do these people dream for, and what will it take to make them happy? Are their dreams attainable, or will they eventually be deferred and dry up "like a raisin in the sun," as Hughes' poem suggests?

SULA

Notes

INTRODUCTION TO THE NOVEL

Sula, Morrison's second novel, focuses on a young black girl named Sula, who matures into a strong and determined woman in the face of adversity and the distrust, even hatred, of her by the black community in which she lives. Morrison delves into the strong female relationships between the novel's women, and how these bonds both nurture and threaten individual female identity. Also, she questions to what extent mothers will go to protect their children from a harsh world, and whether or not these maternal instincts ultimately are productive or harmful.

The novel's structure is circular. When it begins, the narrator is explaining what has happened to the Bottom, the black neighborhood in the Ohio hills above the valley town of Medallion. Medallion's white citizens are moving up into the Bottom and building homes, television towers, and plush golf courses. The Bottom's black residents are moving down into the valley. When the novel ends, the year is 1965, and the narrator tells us more about this neighborhood metamorphosis. In between these chapters, we learn of the events that shape Sula's and the black community's identities between 1919 and 1965.

Sula also explores the life of Nel, Sula's best friend. The girls are best friends, even though they have completely opposite personalities. Sula is impulsive, daring, and independent; Nel, in contrast, obediently does what is expected of her.

When Nel marries, Sula leaves the Bottom and goes to Tennessee, where she attends college for an unspecified amount of time. Ten years later, she mysteriously and unexpectedly returns to the Bottom, but it is immediately clear that she still has the fiery personality she had before she left; she still does the unexpected. And she does more; she does the unthinkable: She places her grandmother, Eva, the family's strong and domineering matriarch, in a nursing home, and she has a brief sexual affair with Nel's husband, Jude. However, a few years later, Sula is near death, and Nel, who hasn't spoken to Sula since she learned of her husband and Sula's indiscretion, visits her old friend and forgives her. Shortly afterward, Sula dies.

The novel is not as concerned with mere story line as much as with the texture of these women's lives and the community they live in. Irony, a literary technique, helps establish this texture. In the prologue, for example, we learn that the hills on which the black neighborhood is situated were once considered worthless land. However, when the whites realized the potential of this land, it suddenly became valuable: They began buying the land, and the blacks were forced to move down into the valley, previously a Whites Only area where they had worked—but were forbidden to live.

Another element of the novel's richness is Morrison's language. Morrison doesn't merely tell us that blacks are being ousted from the Bottom and whites are moving in; she shows us examples of what's being replaced. Workers "tore the nightshade and blackberry patches from their roots"; beech trees are gone, as are the pear trees "where children sat and yelled down through the blooms to passersby." Morrison describes the black women who once leaned their heads back while Irene the beautician lathered their hair; she pictures Reba of Reba's Grill cooking in a hat "because she couldn't remember the ingredients without it."

Morrison enables us to *see* Reba and Irene; we *hear* the nightshade and blackberry bushes being torn from the ground and the children's yelling from the pear trees. We can *taste* Reba's cooking, and we can *feel* the "frayed" edges of men's lapels and the softness of women's felt hats. This is texture. Morrison's prose cannot be skimmed; it must be savored. It is best read aloud, slowly.

LIST OF CHARACTERS

Shadrack

A shell-shocked veteran of World War I from the Bottom, he creates National Suicide Day, January 3, a day every year when people who wish to commit suicide can do so without being stigmatized; this way, death is contained because it occurs only once a year.

Sula Peace

Hannah's daughter and Eva's granddaughter, whose most defining physical feature is a mysterious birthmark over one of her eyes. Although Sula never marries, she takes many lovers; the black community regards her as evil and bewitched.

Nel Wright Greene

The daughter of Helene Sabat Wright, Nel is Sula's best friend—until she discovers her husband and Sula naked on the floor, on all fours "like dogs."

Eva Peace

Although her husband, BoyBoy, deserts her, Eva manages to raise three children. As the matriarch of her family, she runs a large house full of boarders, including the deweys and Tar Baby. She mercifully kills her drug-addicted son, Plum, and possibly her daughter Hannah.

Hannah Peace

Eva's daughter and Sula's mother. An extraordinarily good-looking woman, Hannah has sex with most of the husbands in the Bottom but wants no husband of her own. Because she isn't possessive of their men, the women of the Bottom like Hannah.

Plum Peace

Eva's youngest child and only son; his real name is Ralph, but Eva always calls him Plum. He returns home from World War I a damaged and disillusioned alcoholic and drug addict.

Helene Sabat Wright

The daughter of a New Orleans prostitute, Helene distances herself from her past as soon as possible. After marrying Wiley Wright, she establishes a respectable home and position in the black community for herself and her daughter, Nel.

Jude Greene

Nel Wright's husband. As his biblical name suggests, Jude betrays Nel when he has a one-time affair with Nel's best friend, Sula.

Ajax (Albert Jacks)

The strong, free-spirited young man whom Sula knows during her adolescence. He reappears in Sula's life when she is twenty-nine and becomes her lover for a brief period.

Tar Baby (Pretty Johnny)

A melancholy white man who has come to the Bottom to drink himself to death; he boards with Eva.

Chicken Little

The little boy whom Sula and Nel play with by the river. He drowns accidentally.

the deweys

Three young boys whom Eva takes into her family.

BoyBoy

Eva's errant husband and father to her three children. He deserts the family, then briefly reappears three years later, along with a girlfriend in a pea-green dress.

Mrs. Suggs

A kindhearted neighbor, she helps Eva and her young family after BoyBoy deserts them; she and her husband douse the burning Hannah with water that they are using to can tomatoes.

A BRIEF SYNOPSIS

Just after the end of World War I, Shadrack, a black, shell-shocked veteran, is released from the military hospital where he is being treated for battle stress. Alone and disoriented, Shadrack drifts back to his home in the Bottom, where he becomes known for his eccentricity and for creating National Suicide Day, January 3, a day once a year on which people can commit suicide and not be stigmatized for doing so.

Helene Sabat, the daughter of a New Orleans prostitute, marries Wiley Wright, a man from the Bottom, and establishes a respectable home there. During a journey by train back to New Orleans to visit her ailing, beloved grandmother, she is humiliated by a bigoted white conductor. Her daughter, Nel, watches and vows never to let anyone belittle her so cruelly.

One-legged Eva Peace, her daughter Hannah, and Hannah's child, Sula, live in a large house filled with friends, extended family, and assorted boarders. The matriarchal Eva rules the household from a rocking chair fitted into a child's wagon. Her son, Plum, returns from World War I emotionally wrecked and sinks under his sadness into alcoholism and drug addiction. Eva's devotion to Plum does not allow her to watch him decay, so, after rocking him to sleep one night, she kills him by dousing his bed with kerosene and lighting it.

Sula and Nel begin a friendship and are soon threatened by a gang of harassing Irish Catholic white boys. Sula slices off the tip of her finger as a warning to the boys, and neither she nor Nel is bothered by them again. One day, on the bank of a river, Sula is swinging a little boy named Chicken Little around in circles when he accidentally slips from her hands, lands in the river, and drowns. Sula and Nel tell no one what happened.

Soon after Chicken Little's death, Hannah catches her dress on fire while she is lighting a cooking fire in the yard. From her second-floor bedroom, Eva sees her daughter burning and flings herself out of the upper-story window, hoping to reach Hannah and smother the flames. Hannah dies on the way to the hospital. As Eva, severely hurt by her fall, recovers in the hospital, she remembers seeing Sula standing on the boardinghouse's porch, doing nothing except just watching her mother burn to death.

When Nel marries Jude Greene, Sula leaves the Bottom. Ten years later, she returns, quarrels with Eva, and places her in a nursing home. Shortly thereafter, Nel discovers Jude and Sula naked together and severs all ties with her childhood best friend; Jude leaves Nel and moves to Dayton, Ohio. Sula begins a relationship with a man named Ajax, but he ends the affair when Sula begins acting more like a wife than a lover.

A few years later, Sula is dying, and Nel briefly visits her. When Sula finally dies, she mystically remains conscious: She is outside of her body looking down at it. She realizes that death is painless, something she must tell Nel.

The novel now jumps twenty-five years forward, and Nel is visiting Eva in the nursing home. Eva's mind is disoriented, yet she accuses Nel of complicity with Sula in Chicken Little's death. Nel walks away from the nursing home filled with nostalgic heartache for her longtime friend, Sula, and terrible regret for the long, lost years of her own adulthood.

CRITICAL COMMENTARIES

PART ONE

Morrison begins the novel with a short prologue that focuses on change: the leveling of a black neighborhood—the Bottom, situated in the hills above the valley town of Medallion, Ohio—in order to create a golf course for white people. Years ago, in the 1920s, only white people lived in Medallion and only black people lived in the Bottom; now, the Bottom has become a suburb of the valley town, and the white people who formerly would never have set foot in the black community vastly outnumber their black counterparts.

The Bottom got its name from a cruel trick played on a black laborer by his white farmer boss, who promised the black man that if he'd do some difficult chores for him, he'd receive his freedom and some fertile "bottom land" as compensation. When the work was completed, the white farmer deceitfully told the black man that the bottom land he promised him was actually situated up in the hills overlooking Medallion, but that this particular piece of land was the best because from God's viewpoint it was the "bottom of heaven."

The black man gladly accepted the white farmer's explanation and the piece of land; however, it wasn't long before he realized that the steep, hilly bottom land was cursed with endless erosion and could be farmed only through backbreaking labor and toil.

- *The Bluest Eye* Genealogy
- *Sula* Genealogy

The Bluest Eye Genealogy

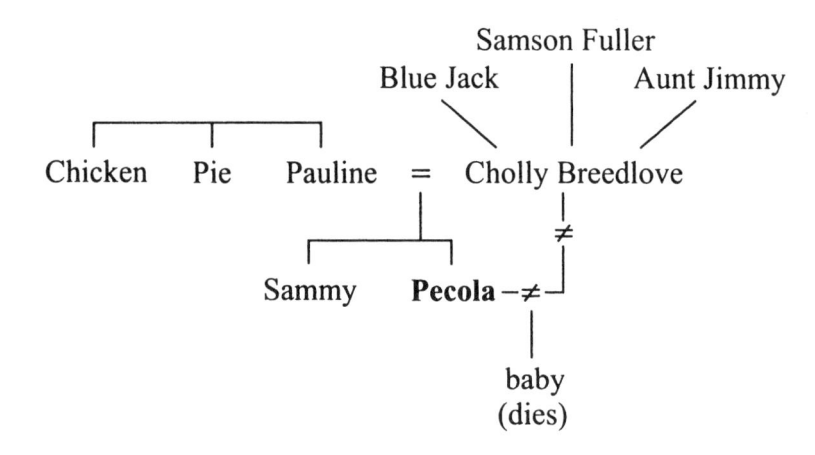

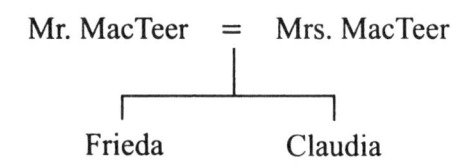

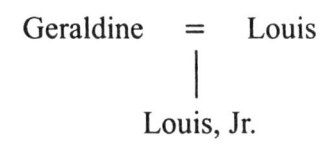

```
                                Samson Fuller
                     Blue Jack  |    Aunt Jimmy
                           \    |    /
   Chicken   Pie   Pauline  =  Cholly Breedlove
                       |                 ≠
                 Sammy   **Pecola** —≠—┘
                              |
                            baby
                           (dies)


            Mr. MacTeer  =  Mrs. MacTeer
                       |
                 Frieda   Claudia


              Geraldine  =  Louis
                       |
                    Louis, Jr.
```

=	married to
≠	has sex with

Sula Genealogy

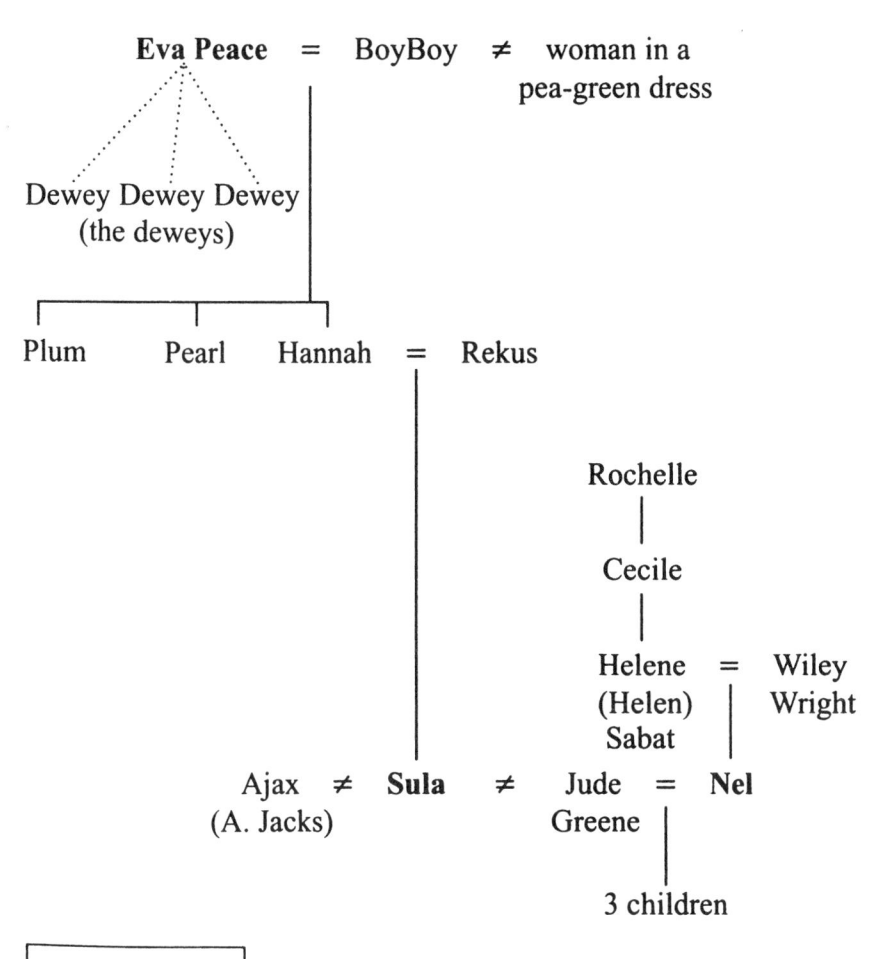

```
         Eva Peace  =  BoyBoy  ≠  woman in a
                                   pea-green dress
       ....../.|.\......
Dewey Dewey Dewey
   (the deweys)

  |        |       |
Plum    Pearl   Hannah  =  Rekus
                   |
                   |                    Rochelle
                   |                       |
                   |                    Cecile
                   |                       |
                   |                    Helene   =   Wiley
                   |                    (Helen)      Wright
                   |                    Sabat
                   |
         Ajax    ≠  Sula  ≠   Jude    =   Nel
        (A. Jacks)           Greene    |
                                       |
                                   3 children
```

=	married to
≠	has sex with
....	caretaker to

Commentary

Morrison's Medallion, Ohio, is an upside-down world. The once-worthless land that a white man jeeringly gave to a black man is now being metamorphosed into a socially desirable locale for white people. But this inverted order is not merely an ironic setting for the novel; it is an essential theme of the novel, for as Morrison has said, "Evil is as useful as good. Sometimes good looks like evil and evil looks like good." What may seem good initially may prove to be not so good after all, and what may seem evil on the surface may later prove to be of value.

The ways that we perceive the ever-changing presence of good and the ever-changing presence of evil are directly related to our shifting opinions of events in the prologue. For example, although it might seem as though bulldozing the Bottom's dusty shacks and replacing them with a swanky golf course epitomizes civic progress, if we listen to Morrison we realize that this now-desirable land will never again be filled with the quality of vibrant life that it once had under its black citizens' stewardship. Country clubs and golf courses are not characterized by the "shucking, knee-slapping, wet-eyed laughter" that once echoed through these hills when the black community lived here.

Humor was especially abundant then, and it even influenced—ironically—the names of businesses—for example, the Time and a Half Pool Hall, which is intentionally humorous and part of Morrison's interweaving of the change/reversal motif. Although the phrase "time and a half" means that someone working at that scale gets more money for working overtime, the men in the pool hall aren't working overtime; actually, they aren't working at all. Another business that is humorously named is Irene's Palace of Cosmetology, a take-off on the names of pretentious beauty parlors—or salons—for rich white women. This particular beauty parlor is hardly a "palace." Palaces are generally associated with rich people, but the only rich people in the valley are the whites who live down in Medallion, not up in the steep-hilled Bottom.

Morrison ends the prologue with a couple of items of suspense: Back in 1920, she says, the black population of the Bottom was wondering what a man named Shadrack "was all about," and what a little girl named Sula "was all about." In fact, the community wondered what it itself was "all about." By beginning at the end,

Morrison shows us what will eventually happen to this laughing, loafing, music-loving, nurturing, close-knit black community, which gains and then loses its identity. The circularity of Morrison's narrative, beginning as it does with the Bottom's end, takes us all the way to the novel's closing sentence, which emphasizes this circular pattern: "It was a fine cry—loud and long—but it had no bottom and it had no top, just circles and circles of sorrow."

(Here and in the following chapters, difficult allusions, words, and phrases are explained.)

- **Nu Nile** a hair product used by blacks.
- **a bit of a cakewalk, a bit of black bottom, a bit of "messing around"** The cakewalk and the black bottom are names of lively dances; messing around is a euphemism for flirting and touching.
- **mouth organ** a metal harmonica, housing a row of free reeds set back in air holes and played by exhaling or inhaling; mouth organs are often used in folk music and sometimes in country-western music.
- **bottom land** The most desirable land that a person can own, true bottom land is rich and fertile and characterized by its dark, loamy texture. In the novel, years of rain and erosion have slowly washed the valuable top soil down from the surrounding hills to the true "bottom," or valley, and created this so-called bottom land, yielding far better crops than what people harvest on the nutrient-poor, hard-to-cultivate soil up in the hills.

1919

Because of a demand for more rooms in the high-risk areas of the veteran's hospital, and because of his violent behavior, Shadrack, a twenty-two-year-old black World War I veteran, is released from the facility where he is being treated for shell-shock; today, the diagnosis would probably be post-traumatic stress syndrome. Alone and disoriented, he painfully makes his way back to Medallion and then to the Bottom, his old neighborhood.

Back at home in the Bottom, Shadrack creates National Suicide Day, the third day of every new year, when he marches through the community ringing a cowbell and carrying a hangman's rope. He tells the Bottom's residents that only on National Suicide Day should people kill themselves or each other, if that is what they desire. Not surprisingly, the townspeople are suspect of Shadrack's sanity, but they soon come to accept his antics and his National Suicide Day, which becomes "part of the fabric of life" in the Bottom.

Commentary

Despite the fact that Shadrack is no longer in combat, he is still overwhelmed by visions in which he sees the horrors of war, and he is especially stunned by the brutal suddenness of death in the midst of battle. In order to counter this specter of unexpectedness, he thinks that if only an entire day could be set aside yearly—a day when people could escape "the smell of death" and the fear of it by committing suicide—then during the rest of the year people wouldn't have to fear death and cower from it. Giving death its own day would compartmentalize it the same way that the food on Shadrack's hospital tray is compartmentalized. On the food tray, there is no chaos: Everything is orderly and within borders. The rice doesn't touch the meat, and the meat doesn't touch the stewed tomatoes. The colors of the foods are distinct and do not mix together.

Shadrack believes that people and things need boundaries to provide order in an otherwise disordered world. For example, although we generally associate straitjackets with insanity, when Shadrack is confined in one he feels secure and protected; he is "both relieved and grateful" because he has a boundary around himself. After he is released from the boundaries of the military hospital, he begins to experience panic—pain, fear, and the hysteria of helplessness. The many concrete walkways that lead from the hospital symbolize the many choices—and dangers—available to him now that he is a civilian again, and the lack of order—"There were no fences, no warnings, no obstacles at all between concrete and green grass . . . "—overwhelms him.. Not until he comes to a town's "regulated" downtown does he finally feel comfortable enough to sit down. The struggle "to order and focus experience" is one of Morrison's main themes in her novel and affects not only Shadrack but all of the characters, including Sula, Nel, and Eva.

After Shadrack's return to the Bottom, the community accepts him as one of their own in spite of his eccentricities. The community knows that he will sell fish twice a week, occasionally get drunk and outrageous, continue to live alone, and, every year on

January 3, celebrate National Suicide Day with a parade. In other words, he will live a very ordered and ritualistic life.

- **running across a field in France** This is a reference to one of many bloody battlefields in France during World War I (1914-18).
- **bayonet fixed** A bayonet is a weapon resembling a short sword or dagger that is attached to the muzzle of a rifle. Shadrack's bayonet is "fixed"—attached to the end of his gun and held forward, ready to stab or thrust into the enemy. During World War I, the U.S. Army used bayonets with 16-inch blades, sharpened along the full-length of the leading edge and along most of the back.
- **private** a noncommissioned soldier in the U. S. Army or U. S. Marine Corps whose rank is below a private first-class.
- **tetter heads** here, teenagers whose heads are pocked with eruptions and itching caused by various skin diseases, such as ringworm, psoriasis, herpes, or impetigo.

1920

Morrison now turns to another resident of Medallion: Helene Wright, whose first sixteen years were spent in New Orleans with her grandmother, Cecile, in a home filled with strict rules and force-fed religious conventionality, and watched over by the authoritative household statue of the Virgin Mary. In contrast, Helene's mother, Rochelle, lived in the Sundown House, a red-shuttered whorehouse, and Cecile watched her granddaughter constantly, ready to squash any evidence that she had inherited her mother's wild blood.

One day, Cecile's great-nephew, Wiley, knocked on her door and met the teenage Helene. He was enchanted with her, married her, and took her North, where they settled into a solid, respectable life in the Bottom.

In this chapter, Helene is taking her daughter, Nel, by train to New Orleans, hoping to arrive before the very old and gravely ill Cecile dies. Although Nel is only ten years old, she is painfully aware of the simmering hate that seethes within the other black passengers on the train as they watch Helene's all-too-eager, ready-smiling attempts to please and appease the loud-mouthed, hostile, white conductor.

Helene and Nel arrive too late; Cecile has already died. Unexpectedly, Nel meets her grandmother, the infamous Rochelle, presumably still a prostitute and still working and living in the Sundown House. The exchange between Helene, her mother, and Nel is very brief, but the trip to New Orleans and the image of her grandmother greatly affect Nel, who appears to gain a stronger sense of self from the experience.

After Helene and Nel's return to the Bottom, Nel befriends a young girl named Sula. At first, Helene is opposed to the girls' friendship—she doesn't respect Sula's mother, Hannah; however, Helene soon grows accustomed to Sula's playing with Nel.

Commentary

In an effort to distance herself as far as possible from what she perceives as her mother's shameless life, Helene marries the right ("Wright") man, keeps a perfect house, and worships in the most conservative black church in the Bottom. Much of her energy is spent trying to smother all signs of creativity and spontaneity in her daughter, Nel. Seemingly, Helene is a model mother and citizen.

When a return to New Orleans to see her dying grandmother seems inevitable, Helene has great misgivings about going south. She's keenly aware of the strict rules of segregation, both written and unwritten. Her best protection, she thinks, is an elegant dress, but when distraction leads her, by accident, into a train's Whites Only car, not even her beautiful brown wool dress can save her from being humiliated by the jeers of the white, racist conductor. Later, she is further humiliated: Because there are no toilets for black people on the train, Helene must substitute fields adjacent to train stations for bathrooms and leaves for toilet paper.

Whereas Helene was able to transform herself successfully into a rigid model of religious and moral respectability in Midwestern Ohio, the South slowly strips her of all her protective veneer. This degeneration begins the moment she steps into the train, when the white conductor addresses her as "gal," a demeaning, stereotypical label that negates Helene's personal identity. The word immediately reminds her of her past, of the whorehouse's red shutters, which symbolize her mother's morally disordered life and behind which Helene was born. She is so personally shaken by this memory—"All the old vulnerabilities, all the old fears of being somehow flawed gathered in her stomach . . . "—that she physically trembles.

During the trip south, Nel sees the exterior of her once-powerful mother slowly disintegrate, and she realizes that, underneath, her mother is weak and vulnerable. She vows that she herself will never be reduced to emotional custard. Declaring that she is a separate and wonderful person, Nel resolves to develop her "me-ness," a transformation that will begin to take shape when she becomes friends with an odd, independent-minded girl named Sula Peace.

- **creole**   In New Orleans, many of the residents are Creole—that is, of mixed black, French and Spanish, and Portuguese ancestry; the Creole language contains a blend of multilingual phrases.
- **dolesome**   sorrowful; filled with grief.
- **a victorious swagger in the legs of white men**   Armistice Day is celebrated annually in November; in Medallion, even though two years have passed since the end of World War I, this military victory is still foremost in the minds of the town's veterans.
- **[Helene] joined the most conservative black church**   During slavery, blacks usually adopted the Baptist church of the slaveholders, infusing their church with Africanisms. After slavery, in an attempt to distance themselves from the spirited, animated black Baptist churches, upwardly mobile blacks sought spiritual refuge in the more refined and quieter Catholic church. Because there isn't a Catholic church in the Bottom, Helene joins the most conservative black church available.
- **gal**   a derogatory term for a black woman; it corresponds to the term "boy" for a black man.
- **Colored Only**   This chapter underscores the South's strict adherence to the laws of segregation. When Helene breaks one of these laws by walking through the Whites Only car of the train, she is sternly reprimanded and could have been arrested had she not apologized profusely and flashed a blindly subservient smile.
- **placket**   V-shaped, overlapping fabric on a blouse, dress, or skirt; the front of a typical rugby shirt has a placket design at the neck.
- **custard**   custard-colored; a mulatto color. It also means something soft and insubstantial, not firm.
- **direc'lin**   directly, or right away.
- **yonder**   over there.
- **head rag**   a length of cloth, often matching the fabric of a dress, that is bound and tied around the head.

- **wrecked Dorics** Morrison likens the white men hanging about the fronts of train stations to the ruins of Doric columns on Greek temples. The men are silent and unmoving, unfunctional and passive watchers.
- **shotgun house** a very narrow house that faces the street, each room opening behind it in a straight line into another room, so that if you fired a shotgun in the front door, the bullet would pass through all of the rooms and exit through the back door.
- **Vrai?** Really?
- **Come, chere** Come here, darling.
- **Comment t'appelle?** What's your name?
- **oui** Yes.
- **'Voir!** Goodbye!
- **pulling your nose** In an effort to make Nel's nose look narrower, sleeker, and more Anglo, Helene tells her to snap a clothespin on it.
- **folded leaves** The reference is to the leaves that Helene has to use instead of toilet paper.
- **goobers** peanuts.
- **read you a dream** interpret a dream.

1921

We meet Eva Peace—mother, grandmother, matriarch. Deserted by her husband, BoyBoy, with three young children to feed, Eva is desperate. Having only a little money and a few beets in the kitchen, she leaves her children with her neighbor, Mrs. Suggs, and promises to return the next day. Eighteen months later, a vigorous and prosperous Eva makes a dramatic return—on crutches and missing her left leg—prompting the black community to speculate as to whether or not she intentionally threw herself under a train in order to collect insurance money.

Eva begins taking in boarders, stray children, and adults whose circumstances are fodder for the town's gossip mill. The mix includes Tar Baby, a troubled, alcoholic white man who is determined to drink himself to death, and three boys, all of whom Eva names Dewey. Eva's daughter Hannah and Hannah's daughter, Sula, move into the boardinghouse. Before long, Hannah begins to enjoy a sweet and flirtatious life. One by one, she collects the town's men as her lovers but never attaches herself to any of them.

After serving a stint in World War I, Eva's son, Plum, returns home. He is an emotionally wrecked, extremely thin and malnourished ex-soldier, a "shadow" who is now addicted to drugs. With the same ferocity that she summoned when she saved his life as a child, Eva burns Plum to death because she knows that he is a doomed, addicted adult: After rocking him to sleep one night, she douses his bed with kerosene and lights it. Her love for him will not allow her to watch him decay into a slowly rotting corpse.

Commentary

Plum is clearly Eva's favorite child; even though he's an adult, she still refers to him as "my baby." She demonstrates such a deep and abiding love for Plum that when she saturates him in kerosene and strikes a match, we accept her heinous crime as an act of desperation born out of love.

In this chapter, there are several references to "top" and "bottom," and "high" and "low" that should be noted. In her house in the hillside Bottom, Eva resides on the top floor, directing the lives of everyone else below. When she sits in her wheelchair, a rocking chair fitted into a child's wagon, children are at eye level with her. Yet because of her matriarchal demeanor and regal bearing, adults who physically tower over her always feel as if they are looking *up* at her.

Eccentric though she is, Eva commands respect from the community. Her eighteen-month absence from her children remains an unsolved mystery, but whatever she did, seemingly it was for the good of the children. Respected as a woman who gets things done, her unusual penchant for taking in strays is peculiar, but it benefits the community's homeless. The community accepts Eva on her own terms, ignoring her disability and gossiping only now and then about it. Unlike Eva's daughter Hannah, who exasperates the women in town because of the number of their husbands whom she has sex with, Eva doesn't threaten the community, even though she dominates people—whether it is during a spirited game of checkers, or renaming children, or deciding on matters of life and death.

- **earthen slop jar** a large-mouthed, enameled container used indoors at night as a toilet.

- **citified straw hat** The reference is to a straw hat worn for purely decorative reasons. Eva might have been able to forgive BoyBoy for having left her with three children to support, but his overly pompous return as a pretentious, quasi-sophisticated "citified" person makes her finally feel inferior enough to be able to hate him thoroughly.
- **a cat's-head stickpin** In southern culinary slang, a cat's-head is a big lumpy biscuit, so BoyBoy's stickpin would probably be large and ostentatious, in bad taste.
- **the *Courier*** The reference is to the *Pittsburgh Courier*, one of the most widely circulated black newspapers at that time.
- **Garret . . . Buttercup** brand names of oleomargarine, a substitute for real butter.
- **bent spoon black from steady cooking** Plum is addicted to heroin; he buys it in solid form and places it on a spoon, which he then puts over a fire in order to melt it into a liquid. Because addicts are usually too shaky to hold the spoon with a pair of pliers until the heroin is liquid and ready for injection, they bend back the spoon handle like a Christmas tree ornament hook and then slip it over the side of a pan in order to keep the spoon steady.
- **dip-down walk** a swagger-like gait, lifting the heels high and rocking for a split second on the balls of the feet before taking the next step; the walk was created by young black males in order to appear sexy and attractive to young women.
- ***Liberty* magazine** a popular magazine of the 1920s and '30s.

1922

The setting of this chapter opens on a cool note—cool weather, a cool wind, and Edna Finch's Mellow House, the town's ice cream parlor—in stark contrast to the ending of the previous chapter, when Plum died in the flames of a kerosene fire, in the heat of Eva's flames of love.

Nel Wright and Sula Peace have become friends, a friendship that will last throughout their lifetimes. In one another, the girls discover their other half; they seem mystically tied to each other's thoughts and feelings. Nel comes from an orderly, tidy home; Sula, from disorder and chaos. Nel's mother is custard-colored; Sula's is sooty. Nel's lighter skin is likened to wet sandpaper; Sula's skin is heavy and brown.

Three events presented in this chapter bond the two girls. When a gang of white, threatening Irish boys confronts Sula and Ned on the girls' way home from school, Sula defiantly cuts off the tip of her forefinger, unnerving the boys and dispersing them. Later in the chapter, the two girls metaphorically explore their inner kindling of early adolescent sexuality by stripping twigs of their bark, peeling out the exposed pulpy center, and then rhythmically digging into the earth with them to create wide, deep holes, which they fill with collected debris and then cover with dirt. Immediately following this scene, a young black boy named Chicken Little joins the girls, and Nel watches as Sula playfully swings Chicken Little around in a wide circle until her hands slip, letting the boy's small body sail through the air and into the river. Chicken Little disappears under the water and drowns.

When Sula sees Shadrack, the mentally unstable war veteran who founded National Suicide Day, on the river's far bank, she runs to his house, hoping to find out if he saw Chicken Little drown. Once she comes face to face with Shadrack, however, she is too frightened of him to say anything. Shadrack's only comment to Sula is the cryptic-like word "Always," which prompts Sula to flee Shadrack's house and seek comfort in Nel's embrace.

Telling no one what really happened to Chicken Little, Nel and Sula sit through Chicken Little's funeral.

Commentary

Friendship with Sula offers Nel a more positive perception of herself. She no longer feels it necessary to "pull her nose," a habit her mother insists that she do in an attempt to make Nel's nose look more sleek and slender, and less broad like her father's. Around Sula, Nel feels thoroughly accepted, especially when the two girls walk the gauntlet of leering young and old black men whom they must pass by on their way to the ice cream parlor. Much to the girls' secret delight, Ajax, one of the young men, sensuously pronounces that the girls are "pig meat." The Bottom's black males are now beginning to view Nel and Sula as young women and no longer as children.

An even greater concern to Sula and Nel than the young black males is the band of white, Irish Catholic boys who continually harass them. As children of newly arrived immigrants, these white Catholic boys are themselves victims of ethnic harassment. Because the town's white Protestants treat them with contempt, they in turn harass Sula and Nel in order to feel superior. However, Sula has had enough; she intends to confront them.

As opposite halves of one another, Nel acts passively, and Sula acts spontaneously and aggressively, always doing the unexpected. Whereas Nel's behavior is solid and consistent, Sula's is unpredictable and disturbing. For example, when Sula slices off the tip of her forefinger as a warning to the gang of white Catholic bullies, the act is not born out of desperation or fear: It is a result of Sula's on-the-spot decision to end, once and for all, her and Nel's victimization by these boys.

Later, when Sula accidentally causes Chicken Little to drown, she is able to cry at his funeral, but she feels no guilt. Nel, on the other hand, feels as though her legs have turned to granite; she feels convicted. Ironically, Nel, the more mannered of the two girls because of her strict upbringing, was the first to harass Chicken Little, and Sula was the one who attempted to protect him by telling Nel to leave him alone.

Sula and Nel's complicity in Chicken Little's death greatly shakes their childhood innocence, although whether or not the two girls are aware of any change in themselves is questionable. Twice after Chicken Little drowns, Morrison writes that there is now "something newly missing" in the girls. Although Morrison never states directly what this "something" is, we come to understand that it is Sula and Nel's innocence, their youthful feelings of invincibility and immortality. Shadrack tries to assure Sula of her permanence when he says "Always" to her, but she is too young and frightened to comprehend his meaning. And Morrison does not completely clarify what Shadrack's "Always" means until the chapter titled "1941," in which she writes that Shadrack said "Always" "to convince [Sula], assure her, of permanency." Nel will finally understand Shadrack's meaning when, at the novel's close, she thinks she hears Sula's spirit blowing through the trees and smells "over-ripe green things," an image of abundance and fruition.

This theme of permanence and immortality is emphasized in the chapter's closing image of butterflies, and Sula and Nel's wondering "what happened to butterflies in the winter." Here, Morrison presents the young girls behaving almost whimsically, as though Chicken Little's death has not affected them in the least. She uses "trotting" and "a summer day" to create an almost idyllic feeling in the girls, who do not know what happens to butterflies in the winter. But we know: The vast majority of butterflies *die* in the winter. Before they die, however, they lay their eggs so that the species will continue and not be completely wiped out. In this way, butterflies ensure their own permanence and immortality, just like Sula does when Nel feels her presence at the novel's end.

- **Camels wrappers**   Camels was a popular brand of cigarettes in this era and one of the few brands available.
- **gabardines**   trousers made out of gabardine, a sturdy fabric of cotton, wool, or twill.
- **voile sleeves**   puffed-out sleeves made from a light, transparent-like fabric.
- **mulatto**   a person of mixed black and white ancestry.
- **keloid scar**   an abundance of scar tissue, common to black skin that is injured.
- **knickers**   puffy pants that gather just below the knees, exposing the calves.
- **Ham's sons**   The reference is to Ham, one of Noah's sons. According to the biblical story, which is often used to justify the persecution of blacks, Noah drank so much wine that he passed out, naked. His son Ham, which in Hebrew means dark or swarthy, discovered him and called on his two brothers to cover their father. Averting their faces by walking backwards toward their father, Ham's brothers covered Noah's nakedness with a cloak. On waking, Noah cursed his son Ham for having seen him while he was naked—nakedness being synonymous with Adam and Eve's Original Sin, according to the Old Testament—and proclaimed that all of Ham's descendants would be slaves. Thus, when the bargeman refers to Ham's sons, he's denigrating all blacks.

1923

One night, the wind begins to roar through the Bottom, shaking houses and felling trees. The community waits for rain, but they wait in vain: The intense, unrelenting wind sucks all of the moisture out of the hills, leaving an oppressive heat wave in its wake.

The next day, Hannah asks her mother if she loved her, Pearl, and Plum when they were children. Eva irritably answers that, as a wife and mother deserted by her husband, she had no time to indulge in loving play with her children: She was too busy nursing them through deadly winters, worms, and contagious diseases, as well as trying to find enough food to keep them alive.

Hannah then asks Eva about Plum's death, and Eva explains that when Plum returned home from the war, he became childlike again. After reliving the painful memory of that bone-chilling winter night when she stood in the outhouse and saved Plum's life by digging out his impacted bowel, Eva then describes how drugs reduced Plum to a baby who wanted, more than anything else, to escape from this fearsome world by crawling back into his mother's womb. Eva decided that before drugs completely destroyed her son, she would relieve his pain by killing him: She first held him close and then set fire to him so that he could die while he was, to some degree, still a man, not a childish, dazed drug addict.

Later that day, Hannah takes a short nap and dreams of a red bridal gown. The next day, she tells Eva about her dream. Eva briefly ponders the dream's significance, but she is preoccupied thinking about Sula's odd behavior of late. Moving her wagon to the window, Eva sees Hannah bending to light a fire in the yard; moments later, Hannah is engulfed in flames. With difficulty, Eva hurls herself out of her wagon and through the second-floor bedroom window, hoping to smother the blaze that consumes her daughter. A neighbor who sees Hannah flailing wildly in flames calls an ambulance. When the ambulance arrives, Hannah and Eva are lifted inside it. Hannah dies on the way to the hospital.

Recuperating in the hospital from the injuries she sustained from jumping out of her window, Eva remembers seeing Sula merely standing on the boardinghouse's back porch, calmly watching her mother perish in the conflagration of flames.

Commentary

This chapter focuses on the importance of omens to the people living in the Bottom. Morrison baits our curiosity by beginning the chapter, "The second strange thing . . . " The *second*? We don't yet know what the *first* strange thing is, but by the end of the chapter Morrison's lengthy list of odd occurrences gives us valuable insights into the intensely superstitious beliefs in the Bottom. These strange things include a choking dry wind; Eva's missing comb, which previously has never been out of place; Hannah's fiery red dress in her wedding dream, superstitiously believed to foretell a death; and Sula's sullen, shifting mood and her shadowy, changing birthmark.

Morrison purposely presents events out of order to highlight the disordered nature of the Bottom. Nothing is the way it should be. Eva identifies the source of this disorder, this evil, in her haunting, matter-of-fact recollection of Sula's passivity as her mother burns to death. She condemns Sula for *watching* as Hannah is consumed by flames, rather than *seeing* her mother as the woman who gave birth to her—and trying to put out the fire that ignites her flesh. Eva implies that Sula has a disturbing, unnatural curiosity about her mother's burning body. All the signs were evident—the dreams, the omens, the coincidences—that prefigured Hannah's tragedy. And, according to Eva, the source of the disorder lies in Sula.

Hannah's death on the way to the hospital is ostensibly the result of fire, but Morrison adds the doubt-raising phrase "Or so they said," which suggests that Eva's maternal altruism might have resurfaced: Rather than have her daughter live out the rest of her life painfully and grotesquely disfigured, Eva, who was placed in the same ambulance as her daughter, might have smothered Hannah. Order and nature are askew here. Recalling the ambivalence surrounding Plum's death, what is evil—Eva's possibly suffocating her daughter—may be good, and what appears to be good might well be called murder—or evil.

After Hannah's death, the community never completely trusts or accepts Sula the way it accepted her mother. The chorus of community women mourn Hannah as a communal treasure; they weep for her "as though they themselves had been her lovers." Hannah may have had sex with their husbands, but she was never threatening or boastful. She was merely unconventional, and, like Shadrack, the community knew what to expect of her. While Hannah was in the natural order of things, Sula is not; Sula shatters order. Eva must face this truth about her granddaughter. Sula did not help her mother; she did not try to rescue Hannah from the fire. She simply stood by and watched her mother die.

- **Kentucky Wonders**   a climbing variety of green beans; the ends of the beans are snapped off by hand and then the beans are snapped in half before cooking. People accustomed to this chore soon acquire speed and proficiency and can snap the pods with rhythmic precision, deftly with one hand.

- **"Give me that again. Flat out to fit my head."** When Hannah asks Eva if she had ever loved her children, Eva is so stunned by the question that she pretends not to understand. She sarcastically asks Hannah to repeat the question in clearer, simpler terms.
- **"You gone can them?"** Eva asks Hannah if she is planning to can the beans. "Canning" is a term used for the storing of cooked fruits and vegetables in sterilized jars that can be kept indefinitely for future use.
- **peck . . . two bushels** A peck is one-fourth of a bushel, or eight quarts; a bushel is four pecks, or thirty-two quarts.
- **stepping tall** acting cocky and impertinent.
- **"we float eggs in a crock of vinegar"** Submerging hard-boiled eggs in vinegar is one way of pickling them for future use. Sarcastically, Eva is chiding Hannah: There were no eggs available for eating while Hannah was growing up, let alone any available for pickling.
- **TB** Tuberculosis is an infectious disease caused by the tubercle bacillus bacteria and characterized by fever, night sweats, and a productive cough. Also called "consumption," it was one of the leading causes of death in the United States until the 1940s, when drugs were discovered to combat it.
- **heifer** a young cow; here, it is a cutting, insulting term.
- **"That straw'll tickle your pretty neck to death."** Before the advent of home freezers, ice was delivered in an ice wagon. The ice was insulated using straw, which would slow the ice's melting. The ice wagon driver warns Mrs. Jackson not to eat the ice so fervidly lest she choke on a piece of straw that might be clinging to it.
- **spigot** a faucet.
- **the number was 522** Playing the numbers was a popular gambling activity. People in the Bottom look for "signs" that tell them which lucky number to play.
- **her nature was coming down** The reference is to Sula's first menstrual period.
- **Somebody else ran to Dick's Fresh Food and Sundries to call the ambulance.** So few people had telephones in their homes that, in emergencies, one had to go to a place of business in order to use the telephone.

- **the colored ward of the hospital** Because of strict segregation laws at the time, black patients were separated from white patients in all areas of the hospital, including the emergency room, regardless of the severity of a patient's injuries.

1927

The novel now leaps forward four years to Nel's marriage to Jude Greene. Just twenty, Jude, a waiter at the Hotel Medallion, craves a job that will allow him to work with his hands and sweat while doing it. When he learns that Medallion is planning to build a new road down to the river, Jude is excited about the prospect of working with other men and establishing a sense of camaraderie with them. Daily, he goes to the job site hoping that he will be picked to work, but the foreman chooses only men who are not black. Enraged, Jude sees his dreams of hard work and male friendship crushed. Nel responds to his vulnerabilities by accepting his marriage proposal.

As the wedding reception begins to wind down, Nel sees Sula leave the party. Although Nel does not know it at the time, Sula is leaving the Bottom and will not return for ten years.

Commentary

Beneath all the chaos and gaiety of the wedding scene is an atmosphere of loss and resignation. One of Morrison's typical reversal scenes, the wedding reception masks the disappointment and rage Jude harbors because bigotry keeps him from his true dream of a better job.

Jude marries Nel not out of love for her, but rather out of anger at not getting the road work. Morrison writes of Jude, "So it was rage, rage and a determination to take on a man's role anyhow that made him press Nel about settling down." Nel accepts his choosing her and thus fulfills her mother's dream of hosting an elaborate wedding and the community's expectation that Nel will assume the traditional female role of wife and mother. With Nel to smooth the rough edges and "shore him up," Jude will shelter her, and "the two of them together would make one Jude." Nel has taken her mother's counsel to heart: She will be good and rub away any glow or sparkle of unpredictability in herself, which the oppressively predictable black community—including Nel's mother—wants her to do.

In marrying Jude, Nel conforms to the community norms and values of social purpose. However, Morrison hints that her conforming as she does actually hurts her; she loses the strong, personal identification—the "me-ness"—that she valued while growing up and befriending Sula. One possible reason that Sula leaves the Bottom immediately following the wedding is that she and Nel can no longer be the inseparable friends they once were. After all, Sula is unpredictable, and Nel has now acquiesced to society's demand that women must marry, have children, and serve their men. Symbolically, Nel's wedding veil is too heavy for her to feel Jude's kiss, suggesting a smothered imagination and eclipsed dreams. Nel has broken the girlhood promise she made to herself to always chase the power and joy and be "wonderful."

Although Sula leaves Nel at the end of the chapter, Nel, whether rightly or wrongly, still feels incredibly attached to her best friend. Morrison writes, "Even from the rear Nel could tell that it was Sula and that she was smiling." Perhaps in the midst of her wedding day's happiness Nel does not realize the significance of Sula's leaving, for she obviously still assumes that she has an almost telepathic link to Sula. However, the chapter ends with Morrison writing that Sula and Nel's next meeting would be "thick with birds," and when we read the opening lines of the next chapter, we find that Sula's returning to the Bottom is accompanied by a *plague* of robins, certainly not a good omen for Sula, Nel, or the black community.

- **cane liquor**   home-brewed liquor made from sugar cane; possibly the cane was barged upriver as a trade item.
- **Black Draught**   (pronounced "draft") a heavy salt concoction sold to poor people, who mixed it with molasses and used it as a tonic and laxative.
- **the Victrola**   a record player, powered by a hand crank.
- **Bert Williams**   In the late 1800s, Williams was a popular black comedian on the vaudeville circuit; he was the first black entertainer to become a major Broadway attraction.
- **tea roses**   roses having a scent resembling tea; they were introduced from China to Europe in 1867. In this country, they have been widely hybridized. The Peace rose is probably the most popular tea rose today.

PART TWO

1937

After an absence of ten years, Sula returns to the Bottom. Looking like a movie star, in a foxtail stole and a black crepe dress splashed with color, she climbs homeward, up to the Bottom. Earlier that same day, the Bottom suffered a bizarre plague of robins, and because of the townspeople's long concern with signs of nature as representing omens, they see Sula's return as a portent of evil, a parallel to the plague of robins.

Sula's reunion with her grandmother, Eva, is extremely confrontational. Sula accuses Eva of burning Plum to death, which causes Eva again to recall seeing Sula's own passive complicity in Hannah's burning to death. Amidst this frenzy of accusations, Sula threatens to douse Eva with kerosene some night while the old woman sleeps. Terrified of Sula's threat, Eva decides to keep her bedroom door locked as long as Sula is in the house.

By April, Sula has assigned herself as Eva's guardian and has committed Eva to a nursing home. The black community is stunned; no one commits family to a nursing home. Now, more than ever, the townspeople are convinced that Sula is evil personified.

Nel and Sula slip back into their friendship with ease, humor, and a deeply satisfying pleasure. Nel questions Sula's decision to place Eva in a nursing home. She tries to understand Sula's fear of the old woman and gently coaxes her to find a better solution for her grandmother. Nel's husband, Jude, is intrigued by Sula's unpredictability and odd philosophy about life.

When Nel discovers Sula and Jude naked together, she realizes that her marriage is destroyed, and that Sula has irreparably ruptured their friendship. Jude abandons his marriage, and Nel suffers deep, emotional trauma over the loss of both her husband and her best friend. Nel's relationships with both Sula and Jude always meant, for her, a fusion of each of these strong, independent personalities with her own timid, less-secure identity; with Sula—and with Jude—Nel was able to create one significant person. After the breakup of her marriage to Jude and her friendship with Sula, she is emotionally shattered and, for a while, seems to be on the verge of emotional despair.

Commentary

In contrast to the other people living in the Bottom, Sula is oblivious to the omens and superstitions that accompany her return. Traditionally, robins are thought of as birds of harmony, bringing peace and the rush of new life and fresh air. Ironically, however, when they are associated with Sula's return, they symbolize her perceived threat to the black community's psychological identity even as their droppings encrust everyone's shoes and the streets of the Bottom. What was once good—robins—has become evil—and all because of Sula. Like the defecating robins, Sula threatens the community's well-being. The girl who left town ten years ago has returned, and her peculiar ways are no longer adolescent whims. They seem like sinister oddities.

In her vicious confrontation with Eva, Sula pulls no punches; her body language positions her on the offensive, and she turns her buttocks to the aging Eva, spitting fire and water at her grandmother's call for pregnancy and blissful "settling." Sula lashes out that she doesn't want to make "somebody else": She wants to make herself. By refusing to settle for the traditional black woman's stereotypical lot in life—wife, mother, and caretaker—Sula inspires Eva's wrath and the community's rancor. Unaffected by the community's condemnation, however, Sula does the unthinkable: She commits Eva to a nursing home, an unacceptable option in the black community.

Why has Sula returned to the Bottom? She has returned out of boredom with the many big cities she traveled through, and because she craves Nel—"the other half of her equation"—and yearns for their girlhood's soulful friendship. Neither Nel nor Sula, however, are girls any longer. Nel is a solid, dependable wife and does what is expected of her. Sula is fluid, spontaneous, and instinctual. On the surface, they seemingly compliment each other and support one another, but Nel senses the atmospheric changes that swept in with Sula, even though their friendship seems to bond them as one.

Both Nel and Sula are sexual women now, and, like the change in the atmosphere, Sula's birthmark begins to change, acting as a metaphor for Sula's shifting appetites. Nel notices that the birthmark has darkened, and Jude sees the defining feature on Sula's face not as a rose, but as a copperhead, or a rattlesnake, both poisonous snakes that recall the serpent in the garden of Eden, which symbolizes sinful behavior. The easy rhythm of these three characters' lives is about to shatter into discord and chaos.

After Nel discovers Jude and Sula "down on all fours naked," the narrative voice shifts from third-person to a dramatic, first-person revelation of Nel's personal disintegration. Nel talks to Jude's "absence" after he leaves, and her pain seems like distilled martyrdom. She has done everything right—she made the conventional sacrifices—but she is left with only loss: "Now her thighs were really empty." Nel thinks that without Jude, her life and sexuality are useless. She agonizingly cries out for someone to confide in, but Sula is no longer available for companionship, and Nel cannot cry as she would like to. She has lost everything that she holds valuable—even her own self-identity.

The images that Morrison uses when describing Nel's inability to cry foreshadow their identical use at the end of the novel. Here, in this chapter, four images dominate Nel's struggle: shifting mud, stirring leaves, the smell of "overripe green things," and a ball of fur. Perhaps most important of these images is the ball of fur, which symbolically hovers just out of Nel's sight—she can see it and touch it if she wants to, but she is afraid of what will happen if she were to focus directly on it. At the end of the novel, these four images are present again, but this time the small ball of fur "broke and scattered like dandelion spores in the breeze," and Nel is finally able to cry out: "O Lord, Sula . . . girl, girl, girlgirlgirl."

What, then, does this odd ball of fur represent for Nel? One possible explanation is that the ball symbolizes the pent-up emotions that Nel has for Sula. Remembering that these two best friends were once inseparable—both physically and, more important, emotionally—while growing up together, when Sula repudiates Nel's friendship by having sex with Jude, Nel is left fragmented; she has lost half of her identity. Only at the end of the novel, when Sula is dead, does Nel come to understand the deep rift in her life without Sula. She finally expresses her repressed feeling for Sula—the ball of fur "broke and scattered"—and realizes that it wasn't Jude she was longing for; it was Sula. Nel is able to cry once again.

- **foxtails**   a stole made of several fox tails linked together.
- **Big Mamma**   a southern term for "grandmother."

- **iceman . . . icebox** People kept perishable items in a wooden icebox that contained large chunks of ice purchased from an iceman.
- **dropsy** refers to the modern-day medical term "edema," which is the accumulation of water in the body's tissues or in the body cavity, giving the body a sagging look.
- **The closed place in the water spread before them.** Morrison uses this phrase repeatedly to refer to death; the phrase recalls Chicken Little's drowning in the river: "The water darkened and closed quickly over the place where Chicken Little sank."
- **hunkies** a disparaging term for a person, especially a laborer from east-central Europe. Here, it includes all white immigrants.
- **copperhead** a poisonous North American snake with a reddish-brown body and darker crossbands on its body.
- **Gabriel Heatter** a radio newscaster.

1939

The black community rallies to defend itself against Sula. She has done the unthinkable: She has put her grandmother, Eva Peace, in a nursing home—for this, she is labeled "roach." In addition, she has had some type of sexual encounter with her best friend's husband and then moved on to other lovers—for this transgression, she is labeled "bitch." Everyone remembers the plague of filthy robins associated with Sula's returning to the Bottom, and they resurrect the old anecdote about Sula's passively watching her mother burn to death; they decide once and for all that Sula's birthmark is really Hannah's ashes. But the most heinous of her crimes is that she has slept with white men. The strong damnation of such an indictment is derived from the racism under which the entire community has suffered. Subtleties of institutionalized racism, coupled with the accepted Jim Crow laws of segregation, remind everyone of the separation of the races. Sula's alleged interracial affairs are perceived as an affront to all of the black people living in the Bottom.

Sula's every move becomes suspect, and even random occurrences of bad luck are attributed to her. Her apparent defiance of physical and moral laws galvanizes the black community against her. Sula is unnatural: she doesn't age, has lost no teeth, never bruises, refuses to wear underwear at church suppers, has never been sick, and doesn't belch when she drinks beer. When she bewitches Shadrack into tipping his imaginary hat to her, the community is convinced that Sula is both the devil and evil personified. Fully aware that she is the town's pariah, Sula does as she pleases, when she pleases.

At the age of twenty-nine, Sula is reunited with Ajax, who, at thirty-eight, becomes her lover. Ajax has heard all of the stories about Sula but is not uncomfortable rebelling against public opinion. The two lovers are drawn to each other's free-spirited independence. For the first time in Sula's life, she realizes that she can express love in terms of permanence and possession.

Sensing a change within Sula as she begins sliding into easy domesticity, Ajax leaves her. Afterward, Sula discovers his driver's license and learns that his name is Albert Jacks—A. Jacks—Ajax. She begins to crumble under the realization that she never really knew him. She crawls into bed holding the crumpled license and dreams a melody, one that states that Sula has sung all of the songs there are to sing.

Commentary

The mounting evidence for Sula being the embodiment of evil is contrived, but this belief gains credibility because Sula refuses to conform to the black community's social norms and tacit laws of acceptable behavior. Despite her two shocking transgressions—placing Eva in a nursing home and committing adultery with Jude—it is Sula's perceived promiscuity with white men that garners the loudest and foulest damnation: She has broken the laws of racial segregation. In contrast, Ajax is accustomed to being contrary to the order of things; as a man, he has license to act as he does without fear of retaliation by the black community. However, as a black woman, Sula's lawlessness alienates and frightens the community, and she is branded accordingly.

Paradoxically, the community-versus-Sula relationship is symbiotic. The previously factional community bands together, defining itself in the face of Sula's shocking behavior. Her rebelliousness unites the community as it moves to protect its own black honor. By identifying Sula as the evil within, the community copes with her the way it has coped with bigotry, misfortune, and oppression—through the collective strength of tradition and a unified sense of neighborhood.

In the midst of the community's swarming and buzzing around this so-called bewitched pariah, Sula takes Ajax as a lover. Never before has she opened her soul so freely to a man. Her lovemaking in the past titillated her "sooty" side and spoke to her wickedness, but for the most part it was lonely and not fulfilling. In the past, she would wait impatiently for her partner to finish and go, to leave her "to the postcoital privateness in which she met herself, welcomed herself, and joined herself in matchless harmony." However, although she finds such psychological singleness powerfully intoxicating, she soon learns that this singleness is actually "soundlessness," a horrible void of nothingness that renders her powerless and, even worse, forces her to confront the possibility of a purely mortal and non-eternal existence.

To combat her fear of loneliness, Sula begins loving Ajax. They meld together into one whole person, much like Nel and Sula used to complement one another. Ironically, Sula's subtle toying with possession and constancy—those value standards that the community treasures and that usually lead to marriage, fidelity, and responsibility—drives Ajax away. Her flirtation with domesticity raises every hackle in his being: Sula is behaving exactly as she earlier condemned Nel for behaving, as a spider "whose only thought was the next rung of the web."

Ajax is in love with Sula's irresponsibility, spontaneity, rebelliousness, and unpredictability—all traditionally masculine qualities. When Sula begins femininely wrapping herself in cologne, Ajax fears that the noose of marriage is waiting in ambush for him, and he takes flight. He moves on, leaving Sula to mourn the loss. Her brief attempt at nesting has accumulated only a crumpled piece of paper with a name on it that she doesn't even recognize. Motherlike, she soothes herself with a lullaby.

- **So they laid broomsticks across their doors at night and sprinkled salt on porch steps.** evidence of superstitions; both counter-measures are believed, by some people, to ward off evil.

- **big Daughter Elk** an important member of the ladies' auxiliary of the Elks, a men's fraternal order.

- **bid whist** a card game similar to bridge.

- **pariah** anyone despised or rejected by others; a social outcast.

- **postcoital** after sexual intercourse.
- **meal-fried porgies** A porgy is a fish; meal-fried means that the fish is fried with a cornmeal coating in hot lard.
- **Jell-Well** a gelatin dessert.
- **Old Dutch Cleanser** a widely sold household cleanser in the 1930s.
- **Tillie the Toiler** a popular comic strip character.
- **bottles of milk** At that time, milk was delivered to homes in bottles with paper lids and left on doorsteps. Ajax steals the bottles of milk that he gives to Sula from a white family's doorstep.
- **working roots** using roots and rites from the occult to gain mystical powers.
- **conjure woman** one who deals in the "spirit" world, or the occult, and works with roots to render spells.
- **Van Van, High John the Conqueror, Little John to Chew, Devil's Shoe String, Chinese Wash, Mustard Seed and the Nine Herbs** These are all ingredients used by conjurers to create spells and tell fortunes.
- **catarrh** inflammation of the mucous membranes, especially of the nose or throat.
- **chamois** a soft leather made from the hide of the chamois, a goat-like antelope native to Europe's mountainous regions.
- **alabaster** Originally, alabaster was a marble used by craftsmen to create beautifully lustered statues; today, alabaster is a granular form of the mineral gypsum, a colorless, white, or yellow mineral. White alabaster is the most highly prized.
- **marcelling irons** irons used to create a hairstyle consisting of a series of even waves put in the hair with a hot curling iron.
- **loam** a rich mixture of moist soil, clay, and sand.

1940

Nel rehearses what she will say to the critically ill Sula, whom she hasn't seen for three years. Motivated by a friendship that once bound them as one, she will visit Sula. Today, she will look down at the stemmed rose on the forehead of her old friend, at the same face that Jude kissed.

The reunion is not extraordinary; minutes later, Nel is off to the pharmacy to fill Sula's prescription, and after Nel returns, the two women settle into a conversation seasoned with innuendoes of what constitutes good and bad, right and wrong. Finally, Nel asks the question that has been tearing at her ever since Jude left: She wants to know why Sula slept with him, an act that severed and destroyed their friendship. Neither repentant nor apologetic, Sula tells her that Jude simply "filled up the space." Nel is crushed that Sula didn't even love Jude. She protests that she has always been "good" to Sula, but Sula points out to Nel the difficulty in separating good from evil. She whispers a final haunting and ambiguous question to Nel, asking her to consider which of them is good and which one is bad. Sula suggests that perhaps *she* was the good girl, and that *Nel* was bad: "I mean maybe it wasn't you. Maybe it was me." Shaken, Nel leaves.

Riddled with pain and drifting into a narcotic limbo of past and present, Sula curls up in her grandmother Eva's bed. Images of Tar Baby and of her mother, Hannah, dance gently within her semi-consciousness, but fatigue grips her. Fetus-like, she draws her legs up to her chest, puts a thumb in her mouth, and remembers that someone once said "Always" to her, but she can't recall who.

Sula stops breathing, and, in this quiet lifelessness, she realizes that she is dead. She thinks of Nel and smiles: Death doesn't hurt.

Commentary

The chapter begins with Nel's exaggerated perception of herself as a "good woman." Since Jude's abandonment of her three years earlier, Nel has lived a hard life, working to support her children and maintain her home. She has done what was expected of her as a deserted wife and mother, and has taken her place with the rest of the women in the community. In the same way that she has been a "good woman," she is, again, a good friend to Sula, whom she never betrayed; Sula betrayed her. Now, she will break the silence and close the gap between Sula and herself.

For the most part, the sickroom conversation between the two women is driven by Nel, who really doesn't know what to say or how to deal with Sula's ambiguity and arrogance. They are at odds, still opposites who, together, form a whole. Nel extols the virtue of hard work; Sula rejects it. Nel blusters about Sula's man-like independence; Sula acknowledges it with pride.

Sula's candor is confrontational as she still refuses to conform—even in dying—to "what every colored woman in the country is doing." They are all, she says, "dying like a stump," while she is "going down like one of those redwoods." Nel, however, clings to what she knows and retorts that Sula has nothing to show for her life but loneliness. Sula's rebellious spirit is fueled by her freedom; any loneliness she has felt is hers alone because she paid the price for her adventures. If Sula is lonely, her loneliness is *hers*. In contrast, Nel's loneliness is made from and dictated by other people; according to Sula, Nel's loneliness, compared to Sula's, is a "secondhand lonely."

As Sula dies, she explores her life one last time. She remembers watching Hannah burn: There was no spite or vengeance within her; she was simply "thrilled" by the sight. The image of her memories scattering like dandelion spores foreshadows the scene at the end of the novel, when Nel finally realizes her love for Sula: "A soft ball of fur broke and scattered like dandelion spores in the breeze."

Sula's final sensory revelation reinforces the theme of friendship. During her final freefall, her thoughts are on Nel. She can hardly wait to tell Nel that dying doesn't hurt.

- **sucked her teeth** a disrespectful sound made by children to show disapproval of an adult request.
- **Lindbergh** (1902-74) Nicknamed "Lucky Lindy," Charles Lindbergh was the heroic American aviator who, in 1927, made the first non-stop solo flight across the Atlantic Ocean. His golden life was tarnished by the brutal kidnapping and murder of his baby son in 1932.
- **Bessie Smith** (d. 1937) An American singer famous for her jazz and blues singing in the 1920s, she was known as the Empress of the Blues.
- **Norma Shearer** (d. 1983) A famous actress of the 1930s, she won an Academy Award for best actress in 1930 for *The Divorcee*.
- **Stepin Fetchit** the stage name of Lincoln Theodore Perry (1902-85), a black comedian famous for playing the buffoon.
- **Clabber Girl Baking Powder** 1930s baking product with a picture of a white girl with blonde hair on the package.

1941

Just as Sula's return heralded superstition and ill omens, word of her death is the best news that the people up in the Bottom have heard in a long time. Her death seems to bring prosperity and promise as the foreman constructing the New River Road tunnel declares that black workers will now be used as laborers. Another sign that Sula's dying has blessed the Bottom is the announcement that a new nursing home will be built and blacks can use the facility; old Eva Peace, Sula's grandmother, will be transferred to the new, clean home. Seemingly, all signs point to the Bottom's dark cloud being lifted now that the bewitching pariah, Sula Peace, is dead.

Hope begins to erode, however, when a sudden and unusual frost settles on the Bottom and ice paralyzes the town for days. Crops are lost and livestock are frozen; women can't get down to the valley to work, and they suffer lost wages; disease grips the young, and despair chokes the rest of the Bottom. Silently and ironically, the townspeople begin to miss Sula, even though they don't realize it. Without Sula as a negative force to be reckoned with—a scapegoat—women don't know where to put their efforts. They don't have to save their children from her wickedness, their husbands are safe from her sexual advances and don't need cuddling, and the women themselves forget why they enjoyed taking care of old people the way they did when they could compare themselves to Sula, who abandoned her grandmother.

On the eve of National Suicide Day, Shadrack is surrounded by loneliness. He looks around for Sula's purple-and-white belt, the only evidence of his only visitor ever in his house. Years ago, a tearful, frightened girl with a tadpole-like birthmark over one eye came to his house. She looked so scared that he tried to comfort her with some words of reassurance, but he could manage only one word: "Always." Then she ran away, leaving her belt behind. For the first time since he began National Suicide Day, Shadrack wants to stay home with the memory of his one visitor.

This year's National Suicide Day is celebrated by many of the townspeople, much to Shadrack's amazement. Scores of people turn out to follow him, strutting, skipping, marching, and shuffling their way through the town, to the tunnel on the New River Road. There, in a frenzy of mob anger and frustration because the tunnel construction jobs have been given to whites rather than to blacks for so many years, the townspeople scramble over the barricade and plunder the construction site. Their fevered pitch of joy and revenge rages, fed by years of oppression, lost wages, and the poverty they have come to accept as a way of life.

Suddenly the tunnel collapses in a wall of water, ice, and mud, killing many of the townspeople, while Shadrack stands high up on the riverbank, ringing his bell.

Commentary

The Bottom community is initially sustained by positive signs of good luck following Sula's death: Construction of the New River Road tunnel will be done by black laborers, and plans are being made for a new nursing home. However, the smug and uncharitable jubilation of the townspeople when they learned of Sula's death is soon hushed by a plague of near-biblical proportion. The weather shifts dramatically, and an omnipotent frost deluges the Bottom with disease, poverty, and cruelty.

Without Sula as a measure of evil, mothers begin beating the children they once protected from her; young people stop caring for the old; and forgotten rifts are rekindled. The community needed Sula to keep it in balance; after her death, people have no way of knowing what is bad in order to do what they think is good.

The tunnel, which initially symbolized freedom from the grips of poverty and bigotry, betrays the townspeople. Ironically, Shadrack reluctantly leads those who rejoiced over Sula's death to the quintessential celebration of National Suicide Day. He stands high on the riverbank, like a prophet ringing his bell on Judgment Day, as he beholds a terrified flock of his community in a scene of sacrifice and judgment.

- **Saffron-colored powder . . . cake of oleo**   The references are to margarine, a cheap substitute for butter; it was first introduced as a chalk-white pliable substance, with the consistency of lard, that was packaged in a plastic bag with a capsule of reddish-yellow dye. When the capsule was squeezed and broken, it released its colored dye, which spread throughout the white margarine. Kneading the plastic bag resulted in a product that eventually resembled butter.
- **Tex Ritter**   the nickname of Woodward Maurice Ritter (1905–73), a country-western singer.

1965

Nearly a quarter of a century has passed. Nel takes stock of the many changes in the community. Blacks are now working in jobs once available only to whites, but Nel is aware of a diminished vitality in people, the same people who previously drew collective strength from their hard times together. The community has spread out and changed, so much so that even the prostitutes seem pale and lifeless compared to the tough, fat, laughing women of forty years ago.

Nel reminisces about the twenty-five years since Jude left. She has spent her life in a tiny sphere of children and work—without love, without marriage. Nel is fifty-five years old, and the future seems to be anywhere but up in the Bottom; blacks are anxious to move to the valley, and whites are erecting television towers and building golf courses up in the Bottom.

Nel visits Eva in the Sunnydale nursing home and is saddened to find a pale, confused miniature of the magnificent Eva Peace she remembers. Their disjointed conversation swings from Eva's non sequiturs to her up-front confrontation about Nel's involvement in Chicken Little's death. Nel pushes the blame for the boy's death solely on Sula, but Eva insists, "You. Sula. What's the difference?" Eva then drifts between the present and the past, but her many references to Nel and Sula being "just alike" haunt Nel, who finally acknowledges that she indeed shares Sula's guilt; perhaps she and Sula really were two halves of the same person.

As Nel leaves the nursing home, Eva calls after her, "Sula?" and Nel hurries away, searching her memory for that day on the riverbank when Sula was swinging Chicken Little. She recalls the good, satisfying feeling she had when she saw his hands slipping away from Sula's, and she remembers feeling proud that she remained calm and controlled while Sula became hysterical.

Nel's walk takes her to the cemetery, where Sula is buried alongside Plum, Hannah, and Pearl. She remembers the day of Sula's death: No one came running at the news of her death, and it was Nel who finally called the mortuary. Besides Nel, only white people came to bury Sula, not like the hordes of black people who showed up for Hannah's funeral. Even Eva refused to come.

Leaving the cemetery, Nel passes Shadrack, who stops and tries to remember where he has seen her. The events of the day well up in her; her eye twitches, and she gazes up at the trees. The breeze carries Nel's whisper, "Sula?" and finally she releases a deep, instinctual cry for her long-lost, beloved friend and soul mate.

Commentary

The narrative has circled back on itself to a time before the prologue was written. Here, the golf course is only a rumor. This final chapter in the novel begins ironically: "Things were so much better in 1965." However, the next sentence reads, "Or so it seemed," and we realize immediately that things are not really better. The Bottom's sense of community is gone—in part, because various advancements of the civil rights movement have fractured the community's unity. Now black people live in the valley in "separate houses with separate televisions and separate telephones"—emphasizing the private and individual space that is so very different from the closeness and the sense of one communal family previously felt in the Bottom.

The narrative then focuses on the current practice of putting old people in nursing homes. Nel also realizes that the Bottom's new prostitutes are "pale and dull," suggesting that blacks have blindly accepted the white community's norms and values. Her uneasiness with these changes foreshadows her move to a new and shocking self-awareness by the end of the day.

Eva, despite her dementia, provides the final revelation of the Nel/Sula friendship theme. She forces Nel to confront her guilt and involvement in Chicken Little's death. For years, Nel has enveloped herself in good works and has done the right things; it was Sula, the bad girl, who let Chicken Little sail toward the river and drown. But Eva insists that there is no difference between Nel and Sula. She draws a vivid parallel as she makes Nel realize that her *watching* Chicken Little drown—and feeling good as she witnessed the tragedy—parallels Sula's *watching* Hannah burn and marveling at her mother's flaming, dancing movements.

When Nel is able to remember the scene on the riverbank so long ago, she finally accepts her dark complicity in the little boy's death. She questions herself about why it felt so good to see Chicken Little disappear under the water and drown. Later, as she stands beside Sula's grave, she discovers that she has denied this perversity all her life. Her own act of cool, evil composure at the river balanced

Sula's anguished goodness, and, afterward, all the rest of Nel's charitable deeds balanced Sula's so-called acts of evil. In spite of death, she and Sula are bonded forever—and the novel closes with Nel keening for Sula.

- **During the war**   Here, the reference is to World War II (1941-45).
- **milk-dull eyes**   eyes dull with age and, quite possibly, with cataracts.
- **so shocked by the closed coffin**   At most funerals in the Bottom, coffins would be open. However, at the funerals of Hannah and Chicken Little, the coffins are closed because of the bodies' mortification. In each case, the closed coffin is mentioned, indicating that a coffin's being closed was not a common occurrence.

CHARACTER ANALYSES

SULA PEACE

Embodying freedom, adventure, curiosity, unpredictability, passion, and danger, Sula takes little from others and gives even less. She is not ruthless; rather, she is spontaneous and unable to moderate or temper the sudden impact her actions might have on her community. She often seems perpetually stuck in a kind of childlike impetuosity. Morrison tells us that Sula "had no center, no speck around which to grow"; her life is like an open rainbow for experimental freedom that often touches the edges of danger.

Sula must experience events in order to reflect on them: She watches her mother burn, she commits her grandmother to a nursing home, and she has a sexual affair with her best friend's husband. As flawed as Sula is, however, she never surrenders to falseness or falls into the trap of conventionality in order to keep up appearances or to be accepted by the community. As Morrison notes of her, "She was completely free of ambition, with no affection for money, property or things, no greed, no desire to command attention or compliments—no ego."

Faced with a racist world and a sexist community, Sula defends herself by creating a life, however bizarre, that is rich and experimental. She refuses to settle for a woman's traditional lot of marriage, child raising, labor, and pain. The women of the Bottom hate Sula because she is living criticism of their own dreadful lives of resignation. Their resentment of her is foreshadowed in the novel's epigraph, from Tennessee Williams' *The Rose Tattoo*, which hints at the independent nature of Morrison's title character. In Williams' play, Serafina delle Rose, an Italian-American woman, mourns for the recent death of her husband, Rosario, who, Serafina's gossipy and cruel neighbors claim, was having an extramarital affair before his death. None of the play's characters understand Serafina's fierce commitment to her dead husband's memory; her questioning his love for her would effectively negate the pride—the glory—she has for herself. Her shallow neighbors think that Serafina has "too much glory," just like the Bottom's black community despises Sula because she has an independence that contrasts to the community's own small-mindedness.

Described by one critic as a "cracked mirror, fragments and pieces that we have to see independently and put together for ourselves," even Sula's birthmark over one eye is perceived differently by different characters. What shape people perceive the birthmark to be says more about them than about Sula. To Shadrack, whose livelihood is catching and selling river fish, Sula's birthmark resembles a tadpole, a symbol of Shadrack's earthy nature and his psychological metamorphosis throughout the novel. To Jude, it looks like a poisonous snake, which recalls the serpent in the biblical garden of Eden and symbolizes the carnal sin that the married Jude commits when he has a sexual affair—however brief—with Sula. To others, including the narrator, the birthmark is a stemmed rose, adding excitement to an otherwise plain face. This stemmed-rose imagery is a positive symbol of Sula's persevering character. She remains true to herself, which Morrison, by linking Sula's birthmark to the image of the traditionally beautiful rose, emphasizes as the most important virtue of a spiritually beautiful person.

As girls, Sula and Nel make up their own rules and define the dimensions of their friendship; together, they are just outside what the community perceives as acceptable behavior: "In the safe harbor of each other's company they could afford to abandon the ways of other people and concentrate on their own perceptions of things." Of the novel, Morrison has said that her motivation for examining female friendship was because too little had been written about women as friends. "If you really do have a friend," she says, "a real other, another person that complements your life, you should stay with him or her. You'll never be a complete person, until you know and remember . . . what life is without that person."

However, as with any relationship, disagreements can occur that test the resiliency of friendship. For Sula and Nel, their separation offers us a chance to see the strength and beauty they find in each other's personality. Sula's sexual encounter with Nel's husband causes a void, a gap, an absence in the women's relationship and allows us to examine what happens when a close friendship is severed. At the time of her death, Sula suffers no limitations; she never betrayed who she is. Nel, however, realizes that she betrayed the "me-ness" of herself in order to have a respectable social position within the Bottom's black community. Any sparkle or vivacity of life she experienced was with and through Sula, and the novel ends with Nel weeping for all of the years she lost while thinking that she was mourning her husband Jude's absence when, in truth, she was mourning for her lost, wonderful friend, Sula.

NEL WRIGHT GREENE

Early in Nel's life, she watches as her mother is humiliated by a train's white, racist conductor; she sees the personal indignity of her mother's having to squat in a field to urinate while in full view of the train's white passengers; and in New Orleans, she realizes her mother's shame at her own Creole mother's life of prostitution. These earth-shattering events in Nel's young and impressionable mind cause her to vow never to lose her own individuality: She will gather power and joy by becoming wonderful. In large part, she accomplishes this goal through her friendship with Sula Peace, a friendship which Nel's mother does not approve of.

Nel's "me-ness," the qualities she vowed to hold onto forever, begins to erode when she marries Jude. In marrying Jude, she is chosen; she does not do the choosing. Acquiescing to his marriage proposal, she hopes that Jude's dreams will become hers. In reality, though, she gives up her own dreams by adopting and authenticating her mother's—and the black community's—traditional ideals about happiness: marriage, motherhood, and religiously sanctimonious piety.

When Jude leaves her, Nel is hollow and suffers under her heavy veil of sacrifice and surrender. She had looked for someone else to design her life and define her dreams; without Jude and Sula, she is spiritless and lost. Morrison hints that Nel's emotional and psychological well-being is close to breaking after Jude abandons her and she abandons Sula, for Nel is left with "no thighs and no heart just her brain raveling away." Stylistically, the lack of any punctuation between "heart" and "just" emphasizes Nel's now-disordered world.

Twenty-five years after Sula's death, Nel realizes that she has wasted all of her opportunities for self-discovery and happiness. In Nel's final moments with Sula, Morrison calls into question the priority of Nel's marriage over her friendship with Sula, for Sula asks of her having sex with Nel's husband, "If we were such good friends, how come you couldn't get over it?" One of the keys to this novel is that friendship supersedes even marriage. Nel finally understands this truth years later when she visits the graveside of her soul mate: "All that time, all that time, I thought I was missing Jude . . . O Lord, Sula . . . girl, girl, girlgirlgirl."

EVA PEACE

Like the biblical Eve, Eva is the mother of all, which explains the number and variety of people living with her in her house. Feeling personally responsible for each of them, Eva frets over the deweys while worrying incessantly about the way the newlywed boarders are treating one another. However, unlike the biblical Eve, Eva takes life as well as gives it: She saves her son Plum's life but later kills him, and she comes close to sacrificing her own life in an attempt to save her daughter Hannah, yet perhaps she smothers Hannah in the ambulance en route to the hospital.

God-like, Eva sits on her makeshift throne in a regal position, appearing to be high above everyone else in her rocking chair atop a child's wagon. The only person in the novel whom Eva succumbs to is Sula, who gains guardianship of her grandmother and then consigns her to a nursing home, an act that outrages the black community, although they can do nothing about it.

CRITICAL ESSAYS

BLACK SOLDIERS IN WORLD WAR I

Much black history is still missing from high school and college history textbooks, and Morrison helps correct that failing in *Sula*, when she introduces Shadrack, a black U.S. soldier fighting in France in World War I.

The war began 1914, but it wasn't until April 1917 that the United States entered the fray. When the country did finally declare war on Germany, the call went out for black volunteers to serve as laborers—building roads, repairing railroads, donating their mechanical skills, and digging trenches. Thousands volunteered immediately. Later, the government asked for black combat volunteers, who were divided into two divisions—the 92nd and the 93rd—made up of black soldiers only; there was no integration of combat troops as there is today. The 92nd division was brigaded by American officers; the 93rd, by French officers.

The "Fighting 369th" regiment, the most famous black regiment in the war, came from the 93rd division, serving under French commanders. The unit fought in France, remaining on the front lines for over 191 consecutive days—never losing a trench, surrendering not even one prisoner, or retreating. After the war, these black combatants were awarded the Croix de Guerre, a French military decoration for bravery in combat.

Not only the French-commanded 369th regiment was decorated, but so also were its fellow regiments within the 93rd division: The 370th was cited for bravery along the Oise and Aisne rivers in northern France, and the 371st and 372nd defended the Argonne Forest in northeastern France so courageously that they also were awarded the Croix de Guerre.

In *Sula*, Shadrack is a World War I combat soldier in one of the country's all-black units, but he does not return as a hero to the U.S. He does not participate in the famous parade up New York City's Fifth Avenue, celebrating the return of the "Fighting 369th." He volunteered to do combat in the war, but he returns home a madman. He doesn't sacrifice his body for his country, a country that wouldn't even recognize his inalienable rights as a human being; instead, he sacrifices his mind. Shadrack returns to the Bottom a mental cripple—so terrified of swift, unanticipated death that he creates a day dedicated to the monster he fears most: sudden, unexpected death, the death that comes without warning.

MOTIFS

Inverted World Order. At the beginning of the novel, the

Bottom is a black community situated atop a hill, above the valley town of Medallion, where the white community lives. Although the Bottom is geographically higher than Medallion, socially and economically the black community is considered lower than their white counterparts, as were all blacks in the early twentieth century, when the novel begins. Ironically, when the novel ends, the black community will have moved down into the valley, and the white people will have bought property and moved up onto the hilltop.

Morrison creates situations in which characters behave differently from what we might expect. For example, in 1927, at Nel's wedding celebration, the old people dance with the young people, and the church women drink the spiked punch. Nel's mother, the staid and conservative Helene Wright, is so calm and relaxed—from drinking—that she doesn't seem to mind the damage being done to her immaculate house by the revelers.

Morrison repeats this theme of inversion by having seemingly negative characters cause positive reactions in people. After Sula's return in 1937, the Bottom's black community abandons its negative ways and adopts positive counterparts. Teapot's previously abusive mother, for example, suddenly becomes caring and nurturing, and women who formerly neglected their husbands now shower them with affection. Ironically, after Sula's death, the old order of negativity returns; the townspeople resume their previous, unhealthy behavior.

Women. With very few exceptions, Morrison's female characters are fiercely independent and subvert the traditionally assigned roles of dutiful wife, mother, and daughter. Of this category, Sula and Eva are the most prominent. Nel, who is raised by her mother to accept without question the passive roles of wife, mother, and daughter, comes to recognize the power of womanhood by the novel's end, although it remains unclear just what she will do with this newfound knowledge.

Sula and Nel come to realize at an early age that because they are neither white nor male, most freedoms and triumphs will be denied them throughout their lives. When Sula returns to the Bottom after having experienced life in many large cities across the country, she notes how dismal the lives of the black women in the community are; she sees "how the years had dusted their bronze with ash," and that "Those [women] with husbands had folded themselves into starched coffins, their sides bursting other people's skinned dreams and bony regrets." Sula's feminist spirit makes her refuse to settle for a woman's traditional lot of marriage and child raising. The Bottom's women hate her because she is the antithesis of their own dreadful lives of resignation. Economically, the women are unable to leave the Bottom, but those who do—like Sula—are likely to return to the black community, for from it they gain the little power afforded them in a racist society.

Sula is the most determined, carefree woman of all the novel's female characters. Her attraction to Ajax originates from her need to have someone more free-wheeling and independent than she. Ajax seems to be the warrior his name suggests, especially when he brings her the bottles of milk. Sula excitedly believes that he must have "done something dangerous to get them," which she greatly appreciates. However, her sole attempt at domesticity sounds the death knell of the relationship. Detecting the scent of the nest, Ajax realizes that Sula is becoming the antithesis of the free-spirited, independent woman whom he was initially attracted to.

Throughout the novel, women's perceptions of love are ambiguous and never clearly defined. For example, to Eva, love is being patriarchally maternal; it gives her license to kill the drug-addicted Plum and possibly Hannah. Eva is the biblical Eve, the mother of all living things, which explains the variety of people living in her home. Although only some of the inhabitants are boarders, Eva still involves herself maternally in their lives. She constantly offers unsolicited advice to new brides on keeping a man. Even with her physical disability, she flirts unashamedly with all the men who surround her. However, these relationships are never consummated, which contrasts to the sexual behavior of her daughter Hannah, who consummates her liaisons with her many gentlemen admirers—and without discretion.

In contrast to Sula's self-assured feminism, Nel represses her self-expression and yields to the oppression of white society and black men. Her loss of Jude results in essentially the loss of her own identity because the vast majority of women of this era believed that a husband gave a woman her place in the community. Growing up, Nel, whose imagination was systematically driven underground by her pretentious and staid mother, Helene Wright, seeks emotional solace from Sula, who defers to no one. The girls rejoice in the sexually charged attention they get from the community's men, who tauntingly call them "pig meat." However, after the dissolution of her marriage, Nel never actively seeks the company of men—giving up after only a few lukewarm attempts at a relationship. Instead, she resigns herself to devoting the rest of her life to her children. She allows herself to be chosen by men, while Sula does her own choosing. By the end of the novel, when Nel cries out to Sula, she laments not only for her long-lost friend, but also for her own wasted potential, recognizing that she has lost the chance to develop into the fullness of her own womanhood.

Racism. The effects of racism upon black American life is a major ingredient in all of Morrison's novels, as she explores the differences between the races' humanity and cultural values. Racism, in all its myriad forms, whether blatant or subliminal, is a part of every scene in *Sula*, with every aspect of the novel expressing some color of racism. Even the laughter of the Bottom is a laughter born of pain—a series of cruel jokes directed against the laughers themselves.

One example of the Bottom's own racism is Helene Wright's concern over her daughter Nel's physical features. Although Helene does not want Nel to be as fair skinned as she is—this so-called advantage can mean trouble in a color-conscious society—she still forces her daughter to pull her nose in order to make it more narrow. And yet Helene herself is the victim of racism, for having grown up in New Orleans, she knows the dangers of breaking Jim Crow laws, the mandates that segregated white society from black. Returning by train to New Orleans for her grandmother's funeral, Helene realizes immediately that she has accidentally stepped over the line that separates the two races when a white conductor catches her in a Whites Only car.

Another example of the white society's racist attitudes occurs later in the novel, when a white bargeman finds Chicken Little's corpse washed ashore at the river's edge. Annoyed at the inconvenience of having to tote the black child's body to the sheriff, the bargeman reacts as though it is not a human life that has been lost. He cannot identify with the blacks of the Bottom as being as human as he is. He even believes that the blacks are so savage that they would kill their own children, which, to him, explains Chicken Little's body being in the river.

In a society that segregates its healthcare facilities, many of which did not allow blacks to step inside their doors, it is not surprising that even those individuals whose skin is white but who have ethnic backgrounds other than Anglo-Saxon are treated better than the Bottom's black residents. One of the key points Morrison makes in this novel is that newcomers—white immigrants—are given preferential treatment for menial jobs, while blacks, with their long history of living in the valley, are mistreated—even by the white immigrants, who, ironically, are themselves looked down on by the established white community; unfortunately, one of the ways that they regain their self-respect is by harassing blacks.

Fire and Water. Throughout *Sula*, the combative elements of fire and water are closely linked to the ever-present motif of death. As a result of the constant references to these elements, the novel projects qualities of creativity and destructiveness that continually transform the images of nature. Among the many motifs, fire is perhaps referred to most frequently.

The first character to die from fire is Plum, whom Eva sets ablaze. The nature of his death is foretold in how he gets high from drugs: His bent spoon is black from "steady cooking." When Plum is burning in his room from the fire that Eva set, it is Hannah who says to Eva, "He's burning, Mamma!" Eva casually responds in false disbelief, "Is? My baby? Burning?" And, on the day that Hannah dies by fire, there is an unnatural, intense heat as Eva rationalizes her role in Plum's burning.

Sula's return to the Bottom after a ten-year absence portends death associated with fire. She confronts Eva and threatens her with the same means of death as happened to Plum, whom Sula knows Eva set on fire. Sula says to Eva, " . . . maybe I'll just tip on up here with some kerosene and—who knows—you may make the brightest flame of them all." Later, when Sula visits Nel, Nel asks her if she wants a cool drink. Sula answers, "Mmmm. Lots of ice, I'm burnin' up," foreshadowing her eventual death by a fever that is described as a "kind of burning." And just prior to Sula's dying, when she wakes from a dream, she is "gagging and overwhelmed with the smell of smoke," although nothing in the house is on fire. Ironically, as Sula dies, she experiences "liquid pain"; she remembers, in death, the promise of a "sleep of water always," and how she would "know the water was near, and she would curl into its heavy softness and it would envelop her, carry her, and wash her tired flesh always."

Sula and Plum are the only characters in the novel who so completely embody the images of fire and water at their deaths. Generally, the women in *Sula* die of fire, traditionally a masculine element, and the men in the novel die of water, a feminine element.

Although his death is from fire, Plum, a passive character, figuratively drowns. As Eva holds him in her arms just before killing him, her face is awash with tears as she remembers Plum as a child in the bathtub, dripping water playfully onto her bosom. Plum, clearly Eva's favorite, is described as having "floated in a constant swaddle of love and affection . . . " Eva immerses him in kerosene, and just before he dies, he perceives that he is floating, womb-like, and drowning. Morrison describes his death, although by fire, as "some kind of wet light traveling over his legs and stomach with a deeply attractive smell . . . splashing and running into his skin . . . Some kind of baptism, some kind of blessing, he thought."

Shadrack is also associated with water, although the biblical Shadrack, in Daniel 3:8–18, is cast into a fiery furnace but emerges unscathed by the flames. *Sula*'s Shadrack, a fisherman by trade, is the only witness to Chicken Little's watery death, and it is he who unknowingly leads many members of the black community to their deaths by drowning. Now living in a shack on the riverbank, when he first saw himself after being released from the military hospital after World War I, he looked into a distorted, watery reflection in water. He wanted water most of all, so much so that when he left the hospital, he immediately sought to know where the river was.

At the end of the novel, many people die of drowning on National Suicide Day, having followed Shadrack to the New River Road tunnel. Tar Baby and the deweys die there, as does Mrs. Jackson, partly because of the ice that she had craved and eaten all her life. Ironically, the hymn "Shall We Gather at the River" will probably be sung at the many funerals to follow, as it was at Sula's.

Another instance of death by drowning is Chicken Little's accidental death in the river. In describing this death, Morrison notes that "the water darkened and closed quickly over the place where Chicken Little sank." The phrase "the closed place in the water" becomes a metaphor for death.

Many minor examples of water associated with men are scattered throughout the novel. These include Nel's father, Wiley

Wright, who is a ship's cook on one of the Great Lakes shipping lines; Ajax's idea of bliss on earth as a hot bath; the deweys' wildly fighting against the threat of being bathed—a fear that foreshadows their deaths by drowning; and, on seeing Hannah burning in the yard, the reaction of Mr. and Mrs. Suggs, who together "hoisted up their tub of water in which tight red tomatoes floated and threw it on the smoke-and-flame-bound woman"—the water puts out the flames, but the resulting steam sears all that is left of the once-beautiful Hannah.

REVIEW QUESTIONS AND ESSAY TOPICS

(1). Use passages and characters from the novel to illustrate how Morrison incorporates the principles and ideals of feminism.

(2). Do any characters change drastically from the beginning of the novel to its end? If so, which ones? Describe their transformations, citing examples from the text to support your answer.

(3). Discuss a decision that a character makes with which you either agree or disagree, and give your reasons.

(4). Choose a character that you would like to interview if it were possible. List the questions you would ask that character, and then write the responses that the character might give.

(5). Who are two of the most memorable characters in the novel? Give the reasons for each of your choices.

(6). Discuss how Nel's grief at the end of the story is, in reality, more for herself than for the death of Sula.

(7). Explain the significance of symbols and omens to the development of the novel's plot.

(8). Discuss Morrison's use of inverted world order in the novel.

(9). Illustrate how the motif of fire and water is threaded throughout the novel.

(10). Typical of Morrison's talent is her ability to weave a magical and musical web of language around an incident of horror. List at least five examples from the novel that illustrate this technique.

SELECTED BIBLIOGRAPHY

GENERAL

BAKERMAN, JANE S. "Failures of Love: Female Initiation in the Novels of Toni Morrison." *American Literature* 52 (1981): 541-63.

CHRISTIAN, BARBARA. "Community and Nature: The Novels of Toni Morrison." *The Journal of Ethnic Studies* 7 (1980): 65-78.

FURMAN, JAN. *Toni Morrison's Fiction*. Columbia: University of South Carolina Press, 1996.

MCKAY, NELLIE, ed. *Critical Essays on Toni Morrison*. Boston: G.K. Hall, 1988.

PEACH, LINDEN. *Toni Morrison*. Ed. Norman Page. London: Macmillan Press, Ltd., 1995.

SARGENT, ROBERT. "A Way of Ordering Experience: A Study of Toni Morrison's *The Bluest Eye* and *Sula*." *Faith of a (Woman) Writer*. Eds. Alice Kessler-Harris and William McBrien. Westport, Connecticut: Greenwood, 1988. 229-36.

TAYLOR-GUTHRIE, DANILLE, ed. *Conversations with Toni Morrison*. Jackson: University of Mississippi Press, 1994.

THE BLUEST EYE

ALWES, KARLA. "'The Evil of Fulfillment': Women and Violence in *The Bluest Eye*." *Women and Violence in Literature: An Essay Collection*. Ed. Katherine Anne Ackley. New York: Garland, 1990. 89-104.

CORMIER, HAMILTON PATRICE. "Black Naturalism and Toni Morrison: The Journey Away from Self-Love in *The Bluest Eye*." *MELUS* 19 (1994): 109-27.

DICKERSON, VANESSA D. "The Naked Father in Toni Morrison's *The Bluest Eye*." *Refiguring the Father: New Feminist Readings of Patriarchy*. Eds. Patricia Yeager and Beth Kowaleski-Wallace. Carbondale: University of Illinois Press, 1989. 108-27.

DITTMAR, LINDA. "'Will the Circle Be Unbroken?' The Politics of Form in *The Bluest Eye*." *Novel: A Forum on Fiction* 23 (1990): 137-55.

DOUGHTY, PETER. "A Fiction for the Tribe: Toni Morrison's *The Bluest Eye*." *The New American Writing: Essays on American Literature Since 1970*. Ed. Graham Clarke. New York: St. Martin's, 1990. 29-50.

FICK, THOMAS H. "Toni Morrison's Allegory of the Cave: Movies, Consumption, and Platonic Realism in *The Bluest Eye*." *Journal of the Midwest Modern Language Association* 22 (1989): 10-22.

GERSTER, CAROLE J. "From Film Margin to Novel Center: Toni Morrison's *The Bluest Eye*." *West Virginia University Philological Papers* 38 (1992): 191-200.

GIBSON, DONALD B. "Text and Countertext in Toni Morrison's *The Bluest Eye*." *LIT: Literature Interpretation Theory* 1 (1989): 19-32.

GRAVETT, SHARON L. "Toni Morrison's *The Bluest Eye*: An Inverted Walden?" *West Virginia University Philological Papers* 38 (1992): 201-11.

KUENZ, JANE. "*The Bluest Eye*: Notes on History, Community, and Black Female Subjectivity." *African American Review* 27 (1993): 421-31.

MINER, MADONNE M. "Lady No Longer Sings the Blues: Rape, Madness, and Silence in *The Bluest Eye*." *Conjuring: Black Women,*

Fiction, and Literary Tradition. Eds. Marjorie Pryse and Hortense J. Spillers. Bloomington: Indiana University Press, 1985. 176-91.

PETTIS, JOYCE. "Difficult Survival: Mothers and Daughters in *The Bluest Eye*." *SAGE* 4 (1987): 26-29.

PORTALES, MARCO. "Toni Morrison's *The Bluest Eye*: Shirley Temple and Cholly." *The Centennial Review* 30 (1986): 496-506.

ROSENBERG, RUTH. "Seeds in Hard Ground: Black Girlhood in *The Bluest Eye*." *Black American Literature Forum* 21 (1987): 435-45.

SULA

BOGUS, S. DIANE. "An Authorial Tie-Up: The Wedding of Symbol and Point of View in Toni Morrison's *Sula*." *College Language Association Journal* 33 (1989): 73-80.

BRYANT, CEDRIC GAEL. "The Orderliness of Disorder: Madness and Evil in Toni Morrison's *Sula*." *Black American Literature Forum* 24 (1990): 731-45.

COLEMAN, ALISHA. "One and One Make One: A Metacritical and Psychoanalytic Reading of Friendship in Toni Morrison's *Sula*." *College Language Association Journal* 37 (1993): 145-55.

DOMINI, JOHN. "Toni Morrison's *Sula*: An Inverted Inferno." *High Plains Literary Review* 3 (1988): 75-90.

GILLESPIE, DIANE, and MISSY DEHN KUBITSCHEK. "Who Cares? Women-Centered Psychology in *Sula*." *Black American Literature Forum* 24 (1990): 21-48.

HOFFARTH, ZELLOE MONIKA. "Resolving the Paradox?: An Interlinear Reading of Toni Morrison's *Sula*." *Journal of Narrative Technique* 22 (1992): 114-27.

HUNT, PATRICIA. "War and Peace: Transfigured Categories and the Politics of *Sula*." *African American Review* 27 (1993): 443-59.

JOHNSON, BARBARA. "'Aesthetic' and 'Rapport' in Toni Morrison's *Sula*." *Textual Practice* 7 (1993): 165–72.

MIDDLETON, VICTORIA. "*Sula*: An Experimental Life." *College Language Association Journal* 28 (1985): 367–81.

MONTGOMERY, MAXINE LAVON. "A Pilgrimage to the Origins: The Apocalypse as Structure and Theme in Toni Morrison's *Sula*." *Black American Literature Forum* 23 (1989): 127–37.

MUNRO, LYNN. "The Tattooed Heart and the Serpentine Eye: Morrison's Choice of an Epigraph for *Sula*." *Black American Literature Forum* 18 (1984): 150–54.

PESSONI, MICHELE. "'She Was Laughing at Their God': Discovering the Goddess Within in *Sula*." *African American Review* 29 (1995): 439–51.

REDDY, MAUREEN T. "The Tripled Plot and Center of *Sula*." *Black American Literature Forum* 22 (1988): 29–45.

SCHRAMM, MARGARET. "The Quest for the Perfect Mother in Toni Morrison's *Sula*." *The Anna Book: Searching for Anna in Literary History*. Ed. Mickey Pearlman. Westport, Connecticut: Greenwood, 1992. 167–76.

SHANNON, ANNA. "'We Was Girls Together': A Study of Toni Morrison's *Sula*." *Midwestern Miscellany* 10 (1982): 9–22.

WESSLING, JOSEPH H. "Narcissism in Toni Morrison's *Sula*." *College Language Association Journal* 31 (1988): 281–98.

NOTES

NOTES

NOTES

NOTES

NOTES

NOTES